What DONALD TRUMP *Means to* AMERICA

**A Black Woman Shares What God Showed Her
about This 45th President of the United State**

Florance McKoy

www.impactcommunications.net

What Donald Trump Means to America

Published by
Impact Communications
P.O. Box 23927
Jacksonville, Florida 32241

www.impactcommunications.net

ISBN: 978-0-9829879-9-5

The author has made every effort to provide accurate Internet addresses at the time of publication, and neither the author nor the publisher assumes any responsibility for changes or errors that occur after publication.

ACKNOWLEDGMENTS

This book would not be possible if it had not been for my Lord and Savior, Jesus Christ, so I first give all glory to Him. I also give special thanks to my husband, Sidney, for being my partner in life and ministry for all these years. Also, I would like to thank all of my colleagues and instructors in ministry who taught me to always give honor to God and to certain institutions even in the way we capitalize certain words; so please excuse any instance where this book does not fully follow those patterns or protocols due to the fact that the publisher has to follow certain rules of grammar and punctuation related to the various editorial guidelines and copyright laws.

CONTENTS

WHY WOULD A BLACK FEMALE DEMOCRAT SUPPORT DONALD TRUMP?

The short, pragmatic answer as to why I, as a black female and former Democrat, am in support of President Donald J. Trump is because I am focused on the big picture of what is best for this nation according to the will of God. But the supernatural answer is that God gave me a prophetic vision that Donald Trump would win the presidency even before he won the Republican Primary—when very few people thought he had a chance. This book will share the story of how God showed me who Donald Trump is and how I actually contacted Mr. Trump and shared my prophetic dream when I had heard he was considering dropping out of the Republican Primary race, and how he took me—a black minister of the Gospel that he didn't even know—seriously.

I am reminded of the scripture from 2 Chronicles 20:20 that says, "Believe in the Lord your God, and you shall be established; believe His prophets, and you shall prosper." This scripture reminds us that when we take God and his true servants seriously, it will cause us to win battles—even the presidency!

And Donald Trump took me seriously and treated me with a lot of respect as I shared with him that God showed me he would be the next President of the United States of America. This allowed me to see that Donald Trump does not take God's servants lightly. This is why there are so many Christians who work with him in the White House, and his vice president, Mike Pence, is also a dedicated Christian.

As for me, in addition to being a former Democrat who is now a registered Republican who serves on the Republican National Committee Presidential Advisory Board as a volunteer, I am first and foremost a minister of the Gospel of Jesus Christ who is licensed and ordained by the church and called by God.

The Bible says, "If my people, which are called by my name, shall humble themselves, and pray, and seek my face, and turn from their wicked ways; then will I hear from heaven, and will forgive their sin, and will heal their land" (2 Chronicles 7:14 KJV). This book is especially written as a call to God's people—those in America who profess to be Christians—to go back to the basics of seeking God and honoring him by obeying his laws. Scriptures like 2 Chronicles 7:14 let us know that the greatest responsibility for the failure or success of this nation is in the hands of the Christians—the church. So judgment must first begin at the house of the Lord, and the church must first repent of its sins of omission and commission before restoration can truly take place in this nation.

Therefore, I am speaking out to tell the Christians about the need to repent of the sin of idolatry that has caused many of them to put their race or political party above God. In terms of political involvement—or lack thereof—the church has its share of repenting to do. In terms of the sin of omission, many in the church are guilty of not exercising the right to vote or not using their voice to speak out in a manner that will help to preserve our Judeo-Christian values and rich Christian heritage. So this book is written to inspire Christian leaders and churchgoers who have not engaged in voting or politics to begin to use their voices and their votes in a manner that will benefit this great nation and honor God.

On the other hand, many in the Christian church are also guilty of voting in a die-hard fashion with blind, obsessive party loyalty for politicians who are godless and immoral. This deceptive and blind spirit must be eliminated from our true Christian churches as much as possible through prayer, repentance, and through proper teaching about politics from a biblical worldview. Whether Democrat or Republican, the laws and values formed by a political party should never be exalted above the laws of God as recorded in his Holy Word. Consequently, this book will also remind Christians not to worship at the altar of any politician or political party.

It is my hope that this book will be a good resource that will inspire people to vote in a manner that is more pleasing to the Lord. As you read this book, I sincerely encourage you to pray for God to teach you his ways and to enlighten you and others regarding how to be a bright and shining light in the midst of our very challenging political environment. With the help of the Lord, the true believers in this country can truly help to make America great again—God's way.

—FLORANCE MCKOY
NORTH CAROLINA

Chapter 1

Did God Really Put Donald Trump in the White House?

I was born in Council, North Carolina, where I grew up in the country on a farm where both parents were devout Christians who were respected in the community and the church. I was the youngest of nine children—and eight of us, including myself, were called into pastoral ministry early in life as young adults. My upbringing caused me to take life seriously, to never hate, and to love everybody regardless of who they were or where they came from or what condition they may have been in.

I was also taught to always accept God's will over man's and to be ready to always do as the Lord instructs us. And even in my younger years as a black woman in North Carolina, I developed a deep desire to help the most underprivileged and less fortunate people in the black community. As one who was involved in street evangelism and pastoral ministry, I had been seeking an answer to a prayer for years for my people, and I was anticipating an answer. So when God showed me Mr. Donald Trump in a prophetic vision, I was open to God's will even though I didn't fully understand it at first.

As an African American woman now in my senior years, the Lord has blessed me with three adult children in pastoral ministry who have been devout ministers since their teenage

years. I have also been blessed with a husband of 35 years
who is a bishop. My whole house serves the Lord, and I told
them about the vision first. And this is a portion of the vision
God showed me in this prophetic dream; when it seemed like
Donald Trump had no chance at becoming president:

> *The Lord God Almighty will put Donald
> Trump in the seat of President of the United
> States and no one will be able to stop or block
> him from the White House, and no one can kill
> him or do him any harm because the Lord will
> place him there. Anyone that comes against
> him will come against God, and the Lord God
> Almighty will fight his battles. His enemies
> that war with him will surely drown in the sea.
> God will use Donald Trump to help the African
> American descendants of slaves in a similar
> way that God used Moses to help the Israelites
> come out of bondage. Donald Trump will also
> help Israel and the Christian church in the
> name of the Lord, and the government of this
> nation shall be upon the Lord's shoulder just
> like it says in Isaiah 9:6.*

I will share more details later. But I had this prophetic
vision about Donald Trump at a time when I was still seeking
answers from God about all the problems and disparities in the
black community. I had been praying for many years: "God
please show me that you are no respecter of persons. Please
show me that you don't love white folks more than you love
black people. Please show me what it is that caused us to be
destitute and not have enough. We seem to be at the bottom of
the totem pole and we can't seem to get help to pull us out."
During the end of President Obama's second term in office,

I was very disappointed because I thought that President Obama, being a black president, would really help the black community. And many people in the black community were so happy about him being the first black president—getting in the seat at the White House. But I and many others felt very disappointed in the end. This caused me to seek the Lord all the more for guidance in terms of the type of person I should vote for in future elections.

The first time he ran for president, I voted for Obama only because he was black, and I had no idea if he had any Christian values. But I didn't vote to support him for his second term because he supported policies that threatened our religious liberties.

And the Lord showed me that it is only the nation that obeys God that can be truly blessed and saved from destruction: because the Bible says "Righteousness exalts a nation, but sin is a disgrace to any people" (Proverbs 14:34 NASB) and "Blessed is the nation whose God is the LORD" (Psalm 33:12 KJV). And a nation is blessed because of its leadership. So when I began to pray all the more, I began to ask the Lord to show me the truth about the state of our nation and African Americans in general.

As I continued to seek God about the condition of our country, I had my second out-of-body experience; but it was not life-threatening like the one I had previously experienced (which I will explain later). I was in a deep trance and I heard the Lord speaking to me and reminding me about all this soulwinning I did over the years, walking the streets for thirty-seven years. And the Lord began to share with me that every person reaps what they've sown. And He said, "because you've been faithful over a little, I'm going to make you ruler over much."

And then the Lord spoke and told this angel to come, and an angel came and anointed my head with oil. I could feel the oil just running down my head. It was as if I couldn't move my neck to look which way the voice was coming. It was like I was paralyzed, whereby I couldn't look to see the voice that spoke with me, but I knew I could hear it and it was like a few words were a thousand messages in my spirit. I mean, I felt the word just filling me with so much understanding and comprehension. When the angel anointed me, my eyes became open, literally open, not just open to look but it was a spiritual sight, and when I got that spiritual sight, I started having visions.

These visions would come on and off, maybe twice a week, for many weeks. And this would all lead up to the time when I had the vision specifically about President Trump. But right before I had the vision about President Trump, I had a vision where I asked the Lord, "Why do our people suffer so much?" I said, "God, please, please tell me," and the Lord did not say one word to me. But about three weeks after that, I was watching television and I put in this movie called the Ten Commandments, and as I was sitting there watching the Ten Commandments depicting the Israelites as slaves to the Egyptians, I heard the Spirit of God speak to me and say: "You are the New Testament slaves and the Israelites were the Old Testament slaves, but God delivered Israel and God's going to deliver you and your people."

That's when I jumped with excitement and I sensed that God's Spirit was leading me to go and study to confirm that the four hundred years Israel was in bondage is similar to the four hundred years that the African Americans have been in bondage as slaves, as ex-slaves, and as descendants of slaves who have faced lots of oppression and some racism even after being delivered from slavery. "But just because you've been in bondage doesn't mean you're not going to come out. If God delivered Israel, God will deliver you all," I sensed the Spirit was saying.

As the days went by, the Lord began to speak to me all the more, and He began to give me the wisdom so I could see things as clear as day. The Lord was revealing to me some very important things that have to be done for black people as a whole to truly come out of servitude and despair: especially in the inner-city, poverty-stricken ghettos in major cities run by Democrats—power-hungry black and white Democrat politicians and church leaders—who are more concerned about their own self-interest and not truly concerned about the best interest of the black community.

As these things became more clear to me, it was then that I had the powerful prophetic dream specifically about President Trump being sent not only to help America, but to also help black Americans in general to come out of servitude, poverty, imprisonment, bondage, and despair. This powerful prophetic vision came to me before he was elected president and at a time when it seemed like he had no chance to even win the 2016 Republican Primary.

During this time, it seemed like just about everybody in the African American community was saying things like: "Oh, he's a bigot, he's prejudiced, and he doesn't like black people, and he is this and he is that." But I was saying to myself, "Lord, I don't know whether to vote for this man or not and I don't know who he is, but I don't believe Hillary Clinton would be able to help us. I just know you told me that it's time for us as black people to come out, but I need to know who's going to help us to come out."

This was when I had that prophetic dream, and in the dream, everybody was saying Hillary is the next president of the United States. And in the vision, the door was right there to the White House, and everybody was saying, "Give it up for Hillary Rodham Clinton, the next President of the United States." And I began to look to see who it was that was coming through the door, and we were waiting for the door to open. When the door opened, it was Donald Trump! And everybody was like, "Oh my God, nobody expected him to win! And how in the world did he win?" Everybody was just going crazy and they were like, "What happened? Hillary had this election?" And when I was looking at Donald Trump come through the door during this prophetic dream, I felt like the Spirit of God was letting me know that God was going to use Donald Trump's background and knowledge as a wealthy billionaire businessman to reach down in the hole to help pull many people out of poverty—including African Americans. A poor man is in the same shoes, so he can't help those who are in poverty and despair, so God will use a knowledgeable, rich man like Trump to reach down in the hole and pull people out.

I was also reminded that just like it took acts of repentance and crying out to God for the Israelites to come out of bondage, African Americans who truly want to be delivered will also need to repent and take full responsibility for their sins. After the Israelites turned away from their sins and came back to God, the Lord sent Moses to deliver them because God uses leadership to bring forth change. In a similar fashion, the Lord showed me that he will use Donald Trump's leadership to bring many more black Americans out of economic despair, but black Americans must also repent of their sins and turn back to God.

When I meditated on these things a bit more, I also reminded myself that it took four hundred years for the Israelites to come out of bondage, and from the time slavery in America began in 1619 to 2019 is four hundred years, and God has already started using President Trump to benefit blacks through his policies that have brought forth prison reform, job creation, low unemployment, opportunity zones for impoverished black communities, and better funding than ever before for black colleges. And God will bring many more black Americans out of servitude as long as they are obedient to the Lord. But we still have a long way to go, because here we are some four hundred years after slavery began in America, and statistics show that whites are currently doing ten times better than blacks in terms of net worth. According to the Federal Reserve, the net worth of a typical white family is $171,000, which is 10 times greater than that of a black family.[1]

In spite of these current statistics, before Donald Trump became president, the Lord had allowed me to envision a positive change for many more black people. And since President Trump has been in the White House, his administration has already begun to help improve the lives of many blacks in America, although our nation has been set back with the coronavirus pandemic.

But when I had that prophetic dream at a time when Donald Trump looked like he had no chance at becoming president, God was beginning to show me that Trump would win the presidency and then do many things that would greatly benefit black Americans. In that prophetic vision, I also need to point out that when the door opened, Mr. Trump didn't come through right away. Everybody was looking for Mrs. Hillary to come through the door, but Mr. Trump was delayed because one of his shoes fell off, and he had to put it back on. And in the vision I saw him putting it back on, and when he came through the door, the Lord was letting me see that he was going to lose a lot by becoming president, and he actually did.

First of all, he gave up his reputation because he has been demonized and ostracized by liberal media and political pundits on both sides of the aisle. He also had to give up opportunities to personally make billions in business, and he gave up his salary, along with giving up his business interests in general. But the Lord let me know that it wasn't going to affect his ability to serve as president because money wasn't in his heart. Donald Trump saw that America was going in the wrong direction and declining in many ways, so he wanted to truly help to make America great again—and this is more than just a slogan to Donald Trump.

In the ensuing days, I shared my vision with all the members of the church congregation and also told many preachers, friends, family members, and associates. But many of them did not want to accept the vision and said things like "that can't be." I said to some of them, "Don't get upset with me about God's vision. I thank God for answering my prayers and sending Donald Trump to help black Americans. Mr. Trump is a rich man like King Solomon and he doesn't need an aggravating job like President of the United States, but he has to sacrifice his great lifestyle for us the same way Moses suffered when he left the comfort zone of Pharaoh's palace." I also told them, "God showed me that He will put Donald Trump in the White House to help us black Americans who are descendants of slaves, because God is no respecter of persons. What he has done for the Israelites He will surely do for us."

I then repeated the details of the prophetic vision to some of my colleagues and explained that in the vision everyone was waiting for the next President of these United States to come through the door in 2016. Everyone said that it was Hillary Clinton because she had the polling numbers of a sure victory, but then the door opened, and in the vision I saw Mr. Donald Trump coming through the door as president.

It was not long after I shared these things with my colleagues that I heard on the news that Mr. Trump was behind all the other candidates in the Republican Primary and was considering dropping out of the race because it seemed like he had absolutely no chance of winning. I then began to think back on the vision I had, and right then and there, something pushed me up out of my seat and said *get in touch with him now, and tell him do not drop out of the race, because God is putting him in the White House to help y'all.* So I decided to contact his campaign as soon as possible. I pulled the campaign information up online, and got the phone number. I called the campaign and I talked to a lady and explained to her that I needed to speak to Mr. Trump and needed his contact information as soon as possible.

Soon after, I actually got to communicate with him. I said, "Mr. Trump, I had a vision about you." I then shared my vision from God and told him, "God would not want you to drop out because God showed me that you, Mr. Trump, will be our next president regardless of what the polls seemed to show." Mr. Trump was actually interested in what I had to say, and he was gracious enough to communicate with me on more than one occasion over the course of several weeks. Ultimately, he respected what I had to say as a black female minister, and he stayed in the race and won as God said. This experience made me feel that Donald Trump has a lot of respect for God and for God's messengers when he believes he is not dealing with a fake or a phony.

I had the privilege of meeting Mr. Trump in person for the first time when he came to my hometown of Charlotte, North Carolina, at the Convention Center on August 18, 2016, while he was campaigning for the presidency. Mr. Trump had personally invited me to this event, and I had the great opportunity to hug Kellyanne Conway, his campaign manager. I got a chance to talk to Mr. Trump and he's a very friendly person; he's business-minded and he's always focused, and I guess that's why he gets so much done. And during that rally —which was several months after I had shared the prophetic vision—it was a blessing to finally meet the man that I knew the Lord had chosen to be our next President of the United States of America.

Now everybody knows the story of how Donald J. Trump began a miraculous surge to win the Republican Primary and defeat Hillary Clinton in the November 2016 presidential election to become the 45th President of the United States.

In a February 2016 news conference several months before Donald Trump won the presidency, even sitting President Barack Obama declared, "I continue to believe that Mr. Trump will not be president. And the reason is because I have a lot of faith in the American people."[2]

President Obama had "faith" that the American people would not vote for Donald Trump. But because God blessed me to have true faith, I got a vision from the true and living God that Donald Trump would be president when Barack Obama and many others thought he had no chance.

My prophetic dream became a reality, and after Donald Trump won the presidential race, he invited me and my husband to come to his inauguration. And we obviously accepted the invitation.

Unfortunately, however, we did not get to witness the entire inauguration. My brother-in-law lives in Washington, D.C., and the weather was really bad, so we went to his house and spent the night so we could try and get to the inauguration on time. But we were not able to do that because the situation in D.C. was so messed up, the parking and all that stuff, and we were not able to get there in time to sit close to all the dignitaries. We did get to see President Trump at the inauguration, but we did not get a chance to interact with him because of our late arrival.

Soon after the inauguration, I was asked to serve on the Advisory Board for President Trump and I answered the call only as a part-time volunteer because of my busy ministry schedule. I am now a registered Republican who serves on the Republican National Committee Presidential Advisory Board. I was a registered Democrat my entire life, and I even voted for President Trump as a Democrat. But then I changed my party affiliation from Democrat to Republican not long after voting for President Trump.

Mr. Trump has also been gracious in inviting me and my

husband on several occasions to eat dinner with him, to come to the White House, to come to Florida, or to come here or there. But I am not able to attend these events because my husband doesn't like to fly, and I don't like to go places by myself, without my husband. And even driving is usually not practical because the drive would just be too far, so unfortunately, we are not able to accept many of President Trump's invitations.

In spite of my limitations, I am glad to be of help to the best of my ability, and I think there will be new beginnings and a turnaround for Christians who have been belittled in this country and for African Americans who have been oppressed, and for Americans in general. Many positive things have already happened as a result of President Trump's strong leadership, but I think even greater justice will prevail under this administration, and I believe that's the reason why God chose a tough leader like Donald Trump to help restore America to greatness—God's way.

God is real, and the fact that He put President Trump in the White House is real. I have since come to realize that there are many confirmations that have come through many other credible spiritual leaders about God's stamp of approval on Donald Trump as the President of the United States. Without me realizing it, while God was speaking to me prophetically in North Carolina about Donald Trump's future as president, the Lord was also speaking to others in different parts of the country and even the world. So Christians especially should be careful not to fight against President Trump, and they should get on God's bandwagon.

Regardless of what man thinks about Donald Trump, God can use anybody he wants to use in the office of President of the United States. Remember how God used Peter in a mighty way after he denied Christ three times? Remember how God forgave King David and called him a man after God's own heart and continued to use him even after David committed adultery and had an innocent man killed to cover his tracks? Remember how God used Moses as a deliverer even after Moses killed an Egyptian and then went in hiding as a fugitive? How about when God converted Saul, the Christian killer, and turned him into the Apostle Paul—the man who wrote most of the New Testament? If God chose all these individuals with sketchy backgrounds and all kinds of imperfections in their lives, who are we to judge Donald Trump if Almighty God chose him to sit in the most powerful seat in the land?

Christians need to wake up and support what God supports and realize that when you think you are just criticizing or fighting against a man's agenda, sometimes you are actually fighting God's agenda. It is okay to constructively challenge any president's policy if we feel he needs greater insight or accountability from his constituents, but Christians especially should stop being so quick to attack or pass judgment on Mr. Trump, and they should pray for him as the Bible commands us to pray for those in authority—especially since there is real proof through prophecy that God put him in office. 1 Timothy 2:1-2 says: "Therefore I exhort first of all that supplications, prayers, intercessions, and giving of thanks be made for all men, for kings and all who are in authority, that we may lead a quiet and peaceable life in all godliness and reverence."

Whose side are you on? It's time to stop being wishy-washy and it's time to stop supporting Democrat leadership that is against our biblical values and against everything that God calls good. It's time for Christians to stop trying to be politically correct like the world, and it's time to take a stand for God and fully support the man He chose to sit in the seat at the White House.

CHAPTER 2

A LONG TIME COMING

My husband and I have spent decades trying to make a difference in some of the most challenging areas in the black community, and at times it seemed like real progress just wasn't being made. But God has shown me through circumstances, visions, and dreams that the season is here for a dramatic change to come for the black community if we will put our trust in him more than we trust in the world system. Yes, it's been a long time coming, but a change is going to come.

In 2017 I had a near-death experience that clearly showed me that God was keeping me on this earth longer because he still had a lot of work for me to do—especially in terms of helping black people in America. It was a dramatic encounter where the doctors told me I had died for about twelve minutes in the hospital after my husband rushed me to the emergency room. I was having palpitations after taking one of the cortisone pills the doctor prescribed. After I got to the hospital, the doctor gave me an IV injection, and at the time I didn't realize it, but my heart stopped and my oldest daughter was with me during this time when I actually died.

Apparently, the medical staff gave me cortisone just to slow my heart rate down, because at the time it was actually beating about two-hundred-and-seventy times per minute. So I went into cardiac arrest but I didn't know it at the time; I just knew I was just sleepy, sleepy, sleepy, and I could barely keep my eyes open. Then I remember just going, and basically it seemed like I was moving as fast as the speed of light. Suddenly I remember experiencing a peace and a solace that was just so awesome.

I had actually died for about twelve minutes—as the doctors would later inform me—and I was experiencing an out-of-body heavenly experience during that time. I didn't fully realize what was going on until the Lord brought me back, but when I was in this zone I was taken in this place and I saw apostles and prophets, and I actually could draw them, that's just how clear it was. And when I went into this place—I don't know where the place was or what it was—they began to talk to me because I tried to kneel down and worship them and they just pulled me up and shared with me that I wasn't supposed to ever do that; I was not ever supposed to worship and honor anyone's flesh but I was to always worship and honor God. And they were telling me things that I was going to do, and I was looking at them and they were saying you are one of us; Don't ever worship us; You're one of us and you've got this great work to do.

Then they said we want you to go back, and I was telling them I didn't want to go back, wherever back was. You don't remember anything. You don't know you've got children. You don't know you've got a husband. You don't know anything about this former life on earth. It's as if your brain has erased everything in this life and there is nothing but solace; you have no worries, you have no frustration, you have none of that. So basically, they were telling me, "Go back." And I was just asking them: "Go back where?" And they kept saying, "Go back, you've got this work to do."

While I still was in this zone, I heard a voice that sounded like someone was in distress. And the compassion in me wanted to help that person. I did not know it at the time, but I was no longer in that heavenly place; I had come back to life on earth and it was my daughter screaming and hollering. I didn't know it was her. I didn't even relate. I just heard a loud, distressing noise that made me want to get to that sound so that I could help whoever it was. I mean, it was so strange because when I woke up—when I first opened my eyes—I couldn't figure out why I was in the bed and why I was there. I was trying to shake myself to figure out how I got there and what was going on. Suddenly within maybe five to ten seconds I recognized my daughter, and she was screaming and hollering with tears running down her face and snot and everything, and the doctors were trying to console her.

While my daughter was panicking, they hit me all in my face and when I opened my eyes the first time, I saw this doctor, but I didn't know who he was at the time. But he was saying to me, "Don't close your eyes." So I finally came to myself and realized that I had gone somewhere and I knew I wasn't the same person. I knew something had changed in me and I knew that there was something that was beyond the comprehension of this life. My husband didn't know I had a near-death experience, and he actually was coming in the room. I knew that God had changed me and my husband was among the first I would tell. My husband was not in the hospital when I passed out because he had gone to park the car after pulling up to the emergency entrance when my heart was beating so fast.

When I woke up in that hospital, the doctors said that I had been dead between eleven and twelve minutes, and they told me I had to stay in the hospital because they needed to check to make sure there were no blood clots in my lungs. They started doing a chest X-ray, and they wanted to put a needle in my naval to try to get any blood clots or clogging. They gave me a handful of aspirin and told me just to chew them. I said, "I don't want to take those aspirin." He said, "Ma'am, you've been dead for at least eleven or twelve minutes. The machine went dead, you had no pulse. You've been dead. We have to do this. Go ahead and chew all these aspirins and we want to do an MRI, and we want to do a scan, and we're going to do a chest X-ray before we move you from the room to make sure your lungs are okay."

Shortly after having this near-death experience, I was in deep thought trying to figure out why I had this encounter, because I had been praying many years for God to answer some serious questions about the condition of blacks in America.

At the writing of this book I am in my late sixties, and I was 66 years old when I had this near-death encounter. The message I got from the near-death encounter—that it was not yet my time to die because I still have work to do—I believe is related to my years of prayers for God to bring greater hope to the oppressed blacks in America. And these prayers relate to a tough question I was asked by a black man on the street many years ago when I was only about 27 years old and doing street ministry. This tough question lingered in my mind for years and I recently got the answer, and God has even shown me that President Donald Trump is a part of the answer.

But I was asked this tough question many years ago when—as a 27-year-old street evangelist—I had gone out one day to do street ministry like always and I asked this black man if he would like to accept the Lord Jesus as his personal Savior.

He said, "If you don't mind, ma'am, can I ask *you* a question?" and I said, "Of course, you can ask." He said, "When you can answer this question, you come back and I'll accept the Lord Jesus as my personal Savior. He said, I'll do it because you're puttin' so much of your time into this." He said "I see you walkin' all the time and I'm sure there are so many things in your life that you could be doing without walking out here in these projects. My question is: Can you tell me that God cares about blacks the same way He cares about whites?"

And so he went on to say, "When you can tell me that God cares about blacks the same way He cares about whites and that God has no respect of persons, when you can tell me that, then I'll accept the Lord Jesus. But until you can tell me that there's no difference between the love of God for blacks as it is for the other people, the Caucasians, I'm not interested in knowing about your so-called God, because every day I wake up and I see how we live and how we are without, and how we have nothing; how we've worked in this country as slaves and yet we're still like slaves, and the whites got everything."

That's what he said to me. So when he said it to me, I went home that night after I had done street evangelism until about 6:30 p.m.; I went home to fix dinner and I literally just broke down and I said, "Lord, you have got to answer this because this man has convinced me that something is wrong. Either we as black Americans are outcasts in your sight, or something changed and we're not aware of the change. But I need to know this, because the fact is if I don't know this, I'm not going back to do any soulwinning any longer because I can't answer these questions. And I want to know if there is a difference because he's not lying; he's actually telling the truth, but the Word teaches me that You are no respecter of persons."

So I started praying about this matter for years; I started back soulwinning, but I started telling people I'm praying for God to make a change in our community and I knew how bad the crime-infested and dilapidated communities were. I knew the slum landlords. I knew all these people that were ostracizing and demonizing blacks and poor people, and it gave me a bad taste in my mouth.

I operated in the area of street ministry for many years, basically going to the neighborhoods all over the country with the most poverty-stricken people and the most crime-infested communities in the projects and similar places. I worked in areas from state to state wherever I was living. While trying to help others, I myself was on limited income, and this was when I worked as a case worker in social services, as well as when I worked for a bank in the accounting department. But on evenings and on Saturdays and Sundays after church, I would go out to try to win souls in the community because I had an unction to try and help the community at large—the poverty-stricken people—because the thievery and crime was so outlandish until I just tried to see what I could do.

Then eventually I started pastoring. My husband and I decided to go into ministry because the fact is that most of the souls we had won, who gave their lives to the Lord, the churches were turning their noses up at them because they were very impoverished. We would even take in the homeless, and my husband used to rent vans every Sunday, and we would drop people off at church so they could go where they could be accepted. We would even rent a hotel room where they could get showers. And we would go to the thrift store on Saturday and get clothes for them to wear so they wouldn't be treated with disrespect by the congregations. So in essence, on Saturday and Sunday we worked like people work on the job. We would run the vans and drop off people—run the vans to the women's shelter, to the men's shelter; we would be all over.

My husband and I noticed that there was so much need. So we even worked on sending one of our daughters to college to get her credentials for early childhood development. Also, we actually mortgaged our house to build a church, and when we did that, we actually opened a child development center with our oldest daughter as the director. She got a state license and we had eighty-seven children on first shift and eighty-seven children for second shift. We would get the members to watch the women's children because we had a lot of single moms.

What we found out is that we seemed to be working all by

ourselves to try and alleviate some of the suffering and some of the cruelty and pain; and I was praying all the time, but it seemed overwhelming at times. I discovered that we needed more than our own efforts to bring lasting change in our black communities; the burdens were too much for me and my husband to carry.

But while my husband and I were trying to serve the black community, we found that many of the single moms did all kinds of immoral things, including prostitution and sleeping around in general, just to keep a roof over their heads and to keep guys doing things for them. And we were working to help them give up that type of lifestyle, but a lot of the women had children by different men and had no child support. It was a vicious cycle. Many of them hadn't even finished their high school education, and most of them started having babies in high school. They had no career skills or trades, so they had to work in low-paying jobs or get on welfare.

So basically we helped get them jobs, and we helped take the children into the child care so they could become independent and not have to rely on sleeping around in order for them to have a roof over their head, or becoming a bed partner and just shacking up with a man so they could pay the rent. My husband went and we bought fifteen passenger vans to pick up the children and pick up the ladies. With the help of God, we were trying to develop Christian character in the people and work on economic development as well so that we could help them improve their lifestyles. We were trying to get them to stop having babies out of wedlock and stop laying around with men and to just trust the Lord.

While helping some of these struggling men and women to buy cars, we learned that most of them had very bad credit. This hindered them in many ways, so we felt we had to do something about this. So my husband and I actually went through the process of establishing our own church's credit union and credit reporting agency that would be especially helpful to low-income people in the black communities. To form the credit reporting agency, I contacted Congress, the Black Political Caucus, and the Trade Commission.

When we got ready to open the credit reporting agency, we were required to come up with a certain amount of funding in order for us to get into the system on the same level with Equifax, TransUnion, and Experian. But we were not able to raise the large amount of capital that was required to get the firewalls and all the equipment and everything we would have needed. We ran into all kinds of obstacles during the process and ended up risking and losing a lot of money without getting fully established. Both ventures—the credit union and the credit reporting agency—were underfunded and lacked the connections we needed to be successful, so we never really got them off the ground.

I am sharing all of these stories about my ministry and business challenges just to clearly show how much I had a heart to help underprivileged people—especially those in the black community. And all of this will eventually lead up to me explaining why I am so grateful for President Trump's efforts to help black people in America.

For the most part, I pursued these business ventures while Barack Obama was President; and I actually pursued the credit union project after things did not work out with the credit reporting agency. I told my husband, maybe we can go on and open up a federal credit union so that we will be able to get money for people to get loans for cars and similar items, so we can do some lending. So we were fortunate enough to get a benevolence finance company established, and it took me two years to fill out all the documents to get the charter for the federal credit union. We had to have about four hundred thousand dollars in capital for the first two years. I had to fight hard because I wanted more than just a state charter, so I got the federal charter so we would be able to serve poor people all over the country, and we operated for two years.

After the two years, we were required to put up another four hundred thousand dollars. And two generous white men that my husband and I knew put up the first four hundred thousand dollars. But we didn't have the four hundred thousand dollars needed for the next two fiscal years because we ran into some complications and challenges because of government orders that prevented us from issuing debit cards and checking accounts to our clientele. So for the first two years we were not allowed to do much of anything because of the government regulations and the massive amount of money we needed to broker MasterCard, Visa, American Express, Discover, and the whole nine yards.

We couldn't make any money, and that's the reason why at the end of two years we didn't have enough capital to stay open for two more years. So in essence, I told them I'm just going to surrender the charter because I'm not going to take anyone else's money to stay open when we had all these restrictions where we couldn't make money.

All of this happened under President Obama's administration, and I found out that having a black president in office did not provide me with any type of real advantage as a black business woman. I learned that if you do not have a certain amount of help from influential individuals with money, there are just some things you cannot do no matter how determined you are—especially when complicated government regulations are involved. Although I am not blaming Obama for my business shutdowns, I certainly have to admit that I was very disappointed that no more help came to black businesses or the black community as a whole.

In contrast, President Donald Trump has already done a whole lot more for the black community in less than one term as president. This is why I believe a leader like President

Trump is an answer to my prayers, because he is using the highest office in the land to make a big impact in the church and the black community. But so many people of all races, including many blacks, are demonizing him and discrediting him in spite of the good things he has done already for the church and the black community, and for America as a whole. I will later explain President Trump's accomplishments more fully, because the far-left, liberal media wants to keep black people ignorant to the good things President Trump has done for blacks as a whole.

Getting back to the credit union, our organization reached out for help under the Obama administration, but nothing came out of it. We were going to open four hundred branches. We had ninety-three hundred churches throughout the country, and their church members were actually going to be a part of the credit union once it got to their state. Before our credit union was shut down, we were fortunate to receive lots of help from an experienced black female banker who was also managing another credit union. It was a white-owned credit union, but she was a black lady working there while she was trying to help us get established. Unfortunately, the credit union she worked for fired her after she had been with them for seventeen years because they apparently viewed her working with us as a conflict of interest, and they also did not approve of how she was going the extra mile to help struggling black customers.

Unfortunately, there are a lot of banks and credit unions that take advantage of poor black borrowers—banks that practice high-interest, predatory lending, and unfair repossessions. A lot of these institutions don't care anything about the people in the poor community and don't really care if they live or die.

I had worked so hard for the community with the credit reporting agency and the credit union and other projects we started, because I was constantly looking for ways to try to pull black people up country-wide. I continued my education in theology until I could start a Bible college to try and get the people of God—especially the black people of God—up out of the hole they were in. I wanted to help in every area where I saw a deficit. I was praying because I was thinking that if God would help the people, then they could see the love of God in our community and God would become more real to them. Through faith in action, I wanted to tell the people, "See, God loves you."

My husband and I even drove around the country for five years putting together a Second Chance Christian Sports League for over thirty-five hundred young, mostly black men between the ages of eighteen and forty in over forty-one states. The purpose of this league was to provide opportunities for these men to earn some extra income using their athletic talents in baseball, basketball, and football—giving them some type of guidance and economic relief so that many of them could take care of their little children.

I knew that if we could help to remove some of the suffering from their lives, that we would have a better chance of getting more African Americans to live holy, righteous lives, instead of living the lives of sinners and backsliders. I knew that in order for us to get a prayer through, we had to be a people that love God and obey his commandments, just like the children of Israel had to obey the commandments in order to go into the Promised Land; and when they didn't obey, they died in the wilderness. I was doing my best to try and get people to see the realness of God. That's why my husband and I have worked so hard with our service to the community.

As I previously stated, God has shown me that this is the season of change—especially for the black community—if we truly put all of our hope and trust in the Lord and obey his commandments. But in order to see the change, many more people in the black community will need to truly get on the Lord's side and stop supporting corrupt politicians who influence the masses to disobey God's commandments. Yes, it's been a long time coming, but a change is going to come.

CHAPTER 3

LET MY PEOPLE GO!

As previously mentioned, after I survived my near-death experience, I was reminded that God did not let me die because he has a very important assignment for me. And part of my assignment is to tell the corrupt liberal politicians to let my people go! In essence, I am also saying to the black community, you must stop having blind loyalty to liberal politicians who have policies that do more to hurt the black community. You must stop voting for politicians just because they are Democrats, and you should only vote for politicians if they support the right policies. Whether Democrat or Republican, you should not support politicians who are ungodly.

After my many years of sacrifice and struggle while trying to help the black community, the event that led me to believe that a real change is about to come relates to the second spiritual dream I had of Donald Trump, and this experience took place after he won the presidency. This was not long after my near-death experience when Donald Trump was already in the White House. In this particular dream, President Donald Trump was holding my hand, and in this dream God was also showing me that Donald Trump is going to have an impact on black Americans similar to the impact that Moses had on the Israelites; because he was going to use his powerful influence as the leader of the United States of America to help many black Americans come out of poverty, bondage, and servitude.

Although a lot of black people don't realize it, they have

been like slaves in servitude to far-left liberal politicians who have controlled many blacks like puppets; and following these blind leaders has caused many black people to fall in ditches. Christians should not be so blind as to follow political leaders who are so contrary and so blind to God's truth. In Matthew 15:14 Jesus said this in reference to blind, hypocritical leaders: "They are blind leaders of the blind. And if the blind leads the blind, both will fall into a ditch."

If you claim to be a Bible-believing Christian and still support these ungodly politicians along with their corrupt policies that promote lawlessness, you are deceiving yourself and you should know better; so you will be beaten with many stripes for willfully going against God's laws if you don't repent. In Luke 12:47-48 Jesus brought out this principle when he said: "And that servant who knew his master's will, and did not prepare himself or do according to his will, shall be beaten with many stripes. . . . For everyone to whom much is given, from him much will be required."

I truly believe that one reason so many blacks are suffering is because they are trusting in corrupt politicians more than God. When people support these corrupt politicians who love what God hates and hate what God loves, reaping and sowing comes into play and "people shall be beaten with many stripes." How can you support politicians who are God haters and who work in the spirit of the antichrist and expect you or your community to be blessed? It's time that we black people wake up and stop selling out to the politicians and instead sell out to God so we can get back in favor with God. In other words, stop following and voting for these corrupt politicians, because this will keep black people in bondage. You can negatively affect the next generation, and even your children can be punished if you continue to support God-haters who make a mockery of his commandments. Deuteronomy 5:9-10 says, "For I, the Lord your God, am a jealous God, visiting the iniquity of the fathers upon the children to the third and fourth generations of those who hate Me, but showing mercy to thousands, to those who love Me and keep My commandments."

So repent of your sins so you can receive God's mercy. This is my message to the black community as a whole. Withdraw your support and stop voting for these corrupt political leaders who support corrupt policies. Many of these politicians are making a complete mockery of God's laws, and Galatians 6:7 says, "Do not be deceived, God is not mocked; for whatever a man sows, that he will also reap."

Many in the black community—and in America in general—have suffered terrible consequences as a result of supporting lawless far-left politicians who promote all kinds of lawless deeds that are totally contrary to the word of God.

The lawless liberal politicians have helped to leave the entire black community in a ditch—a ditch of government dependence and poverty; a ditch of a welfare state that just gives blacks a little bit of crumbs and a bunch of empty promises; a ditch of black-on-black crime that is never solved or even addressed—one ditch after another. A ditch of abortion is killing off the black population, so that other minorities are coming here and getting more powerful and growing greater in number than the black people who helped to build this country through slavery. Blacks are losing job opportunities and are being outnumbered by "new minorities" because far-left liberal politicians are letting all these illegal aliens come through the gate, yet these lawless liberals want to crucify Donald Trump for having good enough sense to build a wall to protect our nation from the constant invasion of illegal aliens that is putting a strain on our country's resources. Consider these facts related to how liberal policies that tolerate a massive amount of illegal immigration negatively impact the black community:

An article from the Washington Examiner stated that "blacks and the working class are punished by decades of illegal immigration." A new report puts the cost of illegal immigration at $113 billion annually and stated that urban blacks are the ones who are burdened most from having to compete with these undocumented aliens for social services and for having to pay taxes to fund free services for illegals. "Once again the Democrats take blacks and poor people for granted. This time they expect us to pay the bills too for their bad ideas," stated Project 21 Co-Chairman Horace Cooper.[1]

"To the political left, illegal immigrants are the 'new blacks.' Thus, its entitlement agenda now prioritizes those who enter our country illegally over the lawful citizens whose ancestors were here and fought for this country as far back as its founding. It's appalling and a disgrace," said Christopher Arps. "What's equally appalling and disgraceful are so-called black leaders who push these policies of unfair wealth transfer. These giveaways to non-citizens must end," he added.[2]

Also, a new National Bureau of Economic Research study suggests that not only does immigration lower wages and decrease employment opportunities for less-educated African American males, but "its effects also appear to push some would-be workers into crime and, later, into prison."[3]

If you put the above statement in the context of *illegal* immigration, it means that a lot of blacks whose ancestors suffered as slaves in this country are losing jobs and other opportunities to people who don't even have a legal right to be in this country—and some blacks, for lack of opportunity, are also tempted to go into a life of crime because of the unfair competition these illegal aliens bring.

The policies of far-left liberal politicians also take away the choice of black parents to send their kids to better schools in better neighborhoods, and they make it almost impossible for horrible teachers to be fired, so the vicious cycle of poorly educated black kids continue.

The black community was also negatively impacted when liberal politicians began creating policies that made it more convenient for black men and women not to get married just to qualify for larger sums of petty government welfare money, food stamps, and other crumbs. These policies enslave black people and destroy the institutions of marriage and family in black communities, and it is time that we black Americans break the curse of this lawlessness by refusing to vote for lawless politicians and by renouncing our affiliation with their corrupt policies. Some of their policies are even designed to punish or persecute people who simply believe in God's plan for traditional marriage between a man and a woman.

It is time for blacks in America to stop trusting in the system and start trusting in God. The curse of ungodly politicians has messed up the black community, and my message to disadvantaged black people is that if you will begin to reject this ungodliness and stand up on your own two feet, you can come out of bondage.

Far-left liberal politicians also promote a culture of death. Think about it—so many of the policies they push on the black community have brought destruction and death. They push abortion—and what does it do? It eliminates the black community by killing black babies, it shrinks us, and it makes us weaker and smaller in numbers. These politicians also push ridiculous, radical global warming or climate change environmental policies that kill jobs, and they push extreme animal rights laws that show more concern for animals than people. To a large degree, a lot of the agendas pushed by these liberal politicians bring death, division, or subtraction. And it is unfortunate that a lot of politicians will sell their soul to get votes. And black people must wake up. I am praying that God will open the eyes of black people all over this country. Lord, let there be an awakening to break the spell of corruption and break the stronghold that black people in America have allowed ungodly politicians to place upon them.

All we need to do—especially those who claim to be Christians—is to stop bowing to the lawless politicians, repent of our sins, and bow to the Most High God, so He can bring true restoration to our lives and our communities. I already shared this scripture, but it is worth repeating because it is the key to receiving help from God in our black communities and in America in general: "If my people, which are called by my name, shall humble themselves, and pray, and seek my face, and turn from their wicked ways; then will I hear from heaven, and will forgive their sin, and will heal their land" (2 Chronicles 7:14 KJV).

It is also disgraceful that many politicians and hateful individuals in liberal media—black and white people—spend a lot of time mocking President Trump and pretending that he has done nothing for blacks in America when the proof is in the pudding.

Although the coronavirus pandemic has set our country back, consider these benefits that have been bestowed upon African Americans due to President Trump's policies in his first term in office: More than one-million new jobs have been added to the economy for African Americans, and many African Americans also received wage increases. There has been less unemployment than ever before among African Americans, with a national black unemployment rate that went to an all-time low of 5.5 percent. It was projected that President Trump's "Opportunity Zones" initiative would generate approximately $100 billion of private investment to help rebuild and invest in underprivileged communities all over the country. President Trump's "First Step Act" criminal justice reform efforts have released thousands of people from jail (90 percent of whom were unfairly sentenced black inmates) and have also helped nonviolent inmates receive training needed to increase chances for success after prison release. And President Trump provided more money than ever before to Historically Black Colleges and Universities when he signed a $360 million grant to support HBCUs—more than America's first black president, Barack Obama, ever allocated.

"These facts are undeniable," stated Pastor Darrell Scott, an African American who is a big Trump supporter and co-founder of the New Spirit Revival Center Church in Ohio. "After all the progress African Americans have made under President Trump, it's difficult to even imagine going back to the Democrats' failed big-government policies that have held us back for so long."[4]

I am in full agreement with Pastor Scott, and I also agree with the young African American author and political analyst, Gianno Caldwell, who stated, "I often say black lives don't matter to Democrats; black votes matter to them."[5]

These are statements from black Americans who have opened their eyes to fully see corrupt political agendas, and they are exposing how deceptive and destructive these agendas have been to the people in the black communities.

For example, while many Democrats are worrying about a very small percentage of blacks being killed by cops, the greater need is to stop African American males from killing each other. But liberals don't want to see that. From 1976 to 2005, 94 percent of black victims were killed by other African

Americans.[6] Nationally, African Americans between the ages of 10 and 34 die from homicide at 13 times the rate of white Americans, according to researchers from the Centers for Disease Control and Prevention and the Justice Department.[7] In other words, young black men are a lot more likely to die than men of other races, and they are the ones who are killing each other off—not the police. This is not just a Republican talking point, as liberals would like you to believe; this is reality in the black community.

And what about the disproportionate number of black men who are imprisoned or involved in the drug trade because they are living with a sense of hopelessness? Nobody looks at that; nobody sees the drug and crime infestation. And nobody's doing anything about it, because leadership has looked the other way.

Many leaders also looked the other way and failed to come to her rescue when Alice Marie Johnson was unjustly sentenced to serve life plus 25 years in prison for a nonviolent drug offense. It was an extremely unfair sentence for a black woman who was a first-time nonviolent offender who had never been in trouble with the law before making the mistake of getting involved with a drug operation. After losing her job at FedEx and facing a series of other tragic events, including a divorce and death of a son, Alice made some wrong decisions while struggling to survive. Although Alice took phone calls that connected drug dealers to one another, she never sold drugs and was not deeply involved in the drug operation as a ring leader. But she faced the very harsh life prison sentence due to mandatory sentencing laws—and in 1996 began serving her time in prison. To this very day, she admits wrongdoing and always takes full responsibility for her actions; but the sentence of life in prison without parole that she was given in 1997 was totally unreasonable—especially from the standpoint that some murderers have been given much lighter sentences.[8]

In spite of the unjust prison sentence, Alice's story has a great ending thanks to the fact that President Trump commuted her sentence to set her free from prison on June 6, 2018, after an appeal from Kim Kardashian West. Alice's is one of the most compelling and dramatic stories that confirms my prophetic vision and demonstrates what Donald Trump means to black America. On the day of her miraculous early release after being commuted by President Trump, a video recording shows Alice with tears in her eyes and crying out with a loud voice on June 6, 2018, saying, "Thank you God and thank you Donald Trump!" After experiencing freedom for the first time in more than 20 years, she declared: "I'm free to hug my family. I'm free to start over. This is the greatest day of my life. My heart is just bursting with gratitude. I want to thank President Donald John Trump. Hallelujah!"[9]

Alice would still be spending life in prison if the Lord had not used President Donald Trump to set her free. More than two years after having her life sentence commuted by President Trump, Alice was featured as a speaker at the 2020 Republican National Convention and she publicly thanked God and Donald Trump for giving her a second chance. "I was once told that the only way I would ever be reunited with my family would be as a corpse," she stated. "But by the grace of God and the compassion of President Donald John Trump, I stand before you tonight and I assure you I'm not a ghost. I am alive, I am well, and most importantly, I am free."[10]

While spending time in prison, Alice was converted and became an ordained minister, and her transformation was described as extraordinary. During her RNC speech, she went on to say: "My Christian faith and the prayers of so many kept hope alive. When President Trump heard about me, about the injustice of my story, he saw me as a person. He had compassion and he acted; free in body thanks to President Trump, but free in mind thanks to the Almighty God."[11]

Toward the close of Alice's RNC speech, she mentioned the profound impact that President Trump's criminal justice reform accomplishments had on her life and on the lives of thousands of others: "Six months after President Trump granted me a second chance, he signed the First Step Act into law. It was real justice reform and it brought joy, hope, and freedom to thousands of well-deserving people. I hollered 'Hallelujah'; my faith in justice and mercy was rewarded. . . . The nearly 22 years I spent in prison were not wasted. God had a purpose and a plan for my life. I was not delayed or denied. I was destined for such a time as this."[12]

In addition to commuting Alice's sentence in 2018, President Trump also granted her a full pardon on August 28, 2020, and now Alice is working with the president to help set many others free from unjust prison sentences. In spite of the kindness and compassion that President Trump has shown to people like Alice and to many others in the black community, a lot of haters still refuse to give him his due credit.

So many of the Trump haters are so ignorant to the point where they don't understand that President Trump is for the downcast. He is for Christianity and he is standing for God's people. God showed it to me, and in that vision, I saw him coming through the door as President before I even knew who Donald Trump really was.

I really only knew his name, and I knew he was a rich man, but I didn't know much more about his life. But I know this: when I was seeking for the Lord to send leadership that would really help black people, the Lord showed me that God had put President Trump in the seat of Moses and he was going to be the one to help African Americans out of servitude. And people think, "Oh no, we ain't been in servitude." But yes, you have. The majority of the people in the black community have been in servitude. Since slavery began in 1619 to 2019 is four hundred years, and we have not made nearly enough progress.

We are still the only race at the bottom. We are still mistreated, ostracized, demonized, and taken advantage of; the giants have taken all our wealth; and we have been in similar shoes as the Israelites in the Bible. But God let me know that he was going to put someone here who could help us, and he showed me the vision of President Trump coming through the door when everybody was saying, "We're votin' for Hillary." And God spoke to me prophetically and said no, she's not going to be president of this country. Donald Trump is going to be the next president, and he showed it to me as clear as day. And in the vision, I saw him come through the door, and the Lord said to me, don't look at his countenance, but look at his heart. His heart is about helping everybody, and he's trying to show everybody that he's got a voice for the weak, he's got a voice for the poor, he's got a voice for the prison inmates, and he's got a voice for even the sinner. He's got a voice for everybody. Many don't want to listen; but he will speak for the entire country.

Moses grew up as a wealthy and influential leader in Egypt who built up Egypt, but he also led God's people out of bondage. So a person can be one to build up the things of the world, and God will take that training and ability to build up the things of God. Moses had to be trained as a shepherd in the wilderness for forty years. The fact is, President Trump was trained in business for many years; he was trained in the understanding of how to make wealth and how to bring people out of servitude from the poverty issues that the African American community is facing, and he didn't make his wealth off the backs of any poor African Americans.

We are dying as a people from thievery and crime, because poverty has besieged us as a people, and we have not increased or progressed enough after four hundred years. Even though slavery was abolished, we have not come out of servitude. We are still the only people who support and make everybody else rich, but while making everybody else rich, we as a people are still poor—making everybody wealthy, making everybody get what they want, making everybody live on the big hills, the big houses, and everything. The politicians who run the big cities full of poor black people are rich, but where are we? Most are still in the slums, still in the ghettos, and still in the place of servitude. We are still paying the slum landlords who are not African Americans. Many are still living with the roaches and the rats.

In some cases, foreigners even come into our communities, start businesses, sell to blacks, make profit, and sometimes don't even respect blacks and view us as outcasts in our own country; white and black music producers get rich making rap music for black rappers with filthy messages that pollute the minds of young people in the black community. We are an exploited people. Even many of the preachers in the black community are in it for their own gain—with a church on every corner—but with no real change taking place in many of the black communities.

We are still living in the bottom of the community of every city, especially the big cities, especially the cities run by far-left liberals. We are still in the same hell holes that we've been in from the beginning. Even in slavery or during the days of segregation, our parents and great grandparents didn't live in this mess, with crime-infested communities filled with blacks killing blacks. After four hundred years, we have not made nearly enough progress as a people. But God is coming to our rescue. I walked the streets for thirty-seven years, trying to get people saved because they didn't have hope. And I came to realize that getting poor people sanctified is challenging. God cares about all these people living beneath poverty, and God often liberates after four generations. From Abraham to Joseph he liberated after four hundred years. Four hundred years for us was 2019. That was 400 years—1619 to 2019—and God showed it to me, so it's time now to come out. We've had our days of being in last place. It's been a long time coming, but a change is going to come. And the time for change is now.

And this is my prayer: "Lord show yourself strong; show the world, the church, and remind everybody that nothing can stand before you or beside you; nothing can overcome the power of God; nothing can withstand the wrath of God; and nothing is greater than the mercy and grace of God." God's got the last move. It might seem like the liberal media controls most of the airwaves, but the Lord can move the liberal broadcasters out and move more God-fearing people in if we speak out and pray. The Lord can even allow his chosen vessels to go on liberal media and speak prophecies that will come to pass in an undeniable way, so that even the liberal will begin to shake in the presence of God. We will not limit the Lord. We will keep praying and believing that the enemies of the Lord will not take over this country, because God's got the last move.

The government is upon His shoulder. He is the Almighty God who can move wicked people out of positions and move the righteous in. The Lord can allow the wicked media companies to go bankrupt and He can flourish the righteous ones all the more. He can allow corrupt leaders to be taken down and He can set up righteous leaders. If we pray that God will confuse and scatter the enemies of the Lord, we can win many more battles if we trust in His strength and not our own.

Proverbs 21:1 says, "The king's heart is in the hand of the Lord, like the rivers of water; He turns it wherever He wishes." He sent Moses to tell Pharaoh to let my people go, and every time Pharaoh's army did something against God's people, God did something far greater to put Pharaoh and his army to shame. A situation is never hopeless as long as God is on the throne and as long as the people of God will stand up for righteousness and seek the face of God.

If you take God out of the leadership of a nation, it will sink. Every enemy in the world would have a much better chance to bring down the United States of America if we forsake God. The fact that the Bible says the government would be upon the shoulders of our Lord Jesus Christ reminds us that the nation that obeys God is the nation that is blessed by God, and the Lord will carry its burdens. Isaiah 9:6 says, "For unto us a Child is born, unto us a Son is given; and the government will be upon His shoulder. And His name will be called Wonderful, Counselor, Mighty God, Everlasting Father, Prince of Peace."

We must remind ourselves that the Lord is still in charge of the universe, no matter how bad things appear at times. 1 Peter 5:7 lets us know we can cast all our cares upon Him, because He cares for you. In essence you could say that when Jesus died on the cross, He took the weight of the world upon His shoulders, and this also reminds us that Isaiah the prophet said "the government will be upon His shoulder."

This reminds us that when we are concerned about all the problems in our world and in our communities, after we do our part, all we need to do is give our problems to Him. The Lord came to set us free from the cares of this world, and He can carry the full weight of all our troubles. The rule and dominion of Jesus, the Son of God, is above all other rule and authority. Philippians 2:9-11 says, "Therefore God also has highly exalted Him and given Him the name which is above every name, that at the name of Jesus every knee should bow, of those in heaven, and of those on earth, and of those under the earth, and that every tongue should confess that Jesus Christ is Lord, to the glory of God the Father."

In Matthew 28:18, Jesus declared that "All authority has been given to Me in heaven and on earth" and Isaiah 9:7 says, "Of the increase of His government and peace there will be no end." Revelation 19:16 says He is "KING OF KINGS AND LORD OF LORDS." Dozens of times in scripture, the Lord is referred to as the "God of Israel," which reminds us that the Lord reigns over all earthly governments!

CHAPTER 4

WHOSE SIDE
ARE YOU ON?

In this chapter I especially want to bring out the point that if you are a God-fearing American who loves this country, you must pick a side—must make a choice—and determine whose side you are on if you have not done so already. You must choose good or evil. You must choose God or corrupt, ungodly political leadership. There is no middle ground. There is no in-between. There is no straddling the fence. The destiny and the soul of this nation is at stake; so whose side are you on?

If you truly have a conscience and if you truly know God, you must not vote for an ungodly politician and you must not give blind loyalty to any political party—Democrat or Republican. If you support a political party and give them your vote when that party has policies that go against God's commandments—especially in the presidential election—I would go as far to say that you are working against God.

If you truly want to have the freedom to live your life according to God's laws, you have to vote for the presidential candidate who is more closely aligned with biblical values. President Trump is the leader who is committed to protecting our religious freedoms as Americans. Not only has God given prophetic proof that Donald Trump has been chosen to be President of the United States of America for such a time as this, but the writing is on the wall.

Black Christians especially need to tell their friends, family, and the wilderness church members to stop being brainwashed by the far-left politicians who will allow illegal immigrants to come in and kill job opportunities in the black community. These liberal politicians don't believe in having a wall built to protect our country's borders, when common sense lets us know that not having a wall built to keep out illegal aliens makes it much easier for drug dealers and terrorists to sneak into our country to commit crimes that lead to death and destruction. These far-left politicians are also letting communities get looted and burned by rioters who have also murdered many people during these violent protests related to the death of George Floyd.

Also, these politicians takes millions of your tax dollars and my tax dollars to fund Planned Parenthood so they can continue to kill off our black babies through abortion on demand, while you as Christians help pay for their sinful acts. The Holy Scriptures tell us not to be partakers of other men's sins. If you don't think abortion is murder, then go online and do a search for "pictures of aborted babies"; you will have no doubt in your mind that abortion is the murder of innocent babies. So blacks must stop voting for these liberal politicians who support these destructive policies.

So I ask the question again: whose side are you on? This is our time to come out if we choose life rather than death. In Matthew 12:30 Jesus said, "He who is not with Me is against Me," so there is no middle ground. You must make a choice. Everybody that's not on the Lord's side, that stands with corrupt politicians who promote ungodly agendas, has opened up the door for curses to come upon them and their families—because God is not mocked. And everybody that stands on the Lord's side, with the political leaders who reverence God and His laws, can have blessings and length of days.

Deuteronomy 30:15-20 says, "See, I have set before you

today life and good, death and evil, in that I command you today to love the Lord your God, to walk in His ways, and to keep His commandments, His statutes, and His judgments, that you may live and multiply. . . . I call heaven and earth as witnesses today against you, that I have set before you life and death, blessing and cursing; therefore choose life, that both you and your descendants may live; that you may love the Lord your God, that you may obey His voice, and that you may cling to Him, for He is your life and the length of your days."

Choose life over death the next time you vote. We have to make the right choice. We have to choose Christ over everything else. And if we can't choose Christ over everything else, we've been deceived by the spirit of the antichrist which controls many of these far-left politicians. And if you claim to be a Christian or a person who has any reverence for God at all, how can you support their culture of death?

Jesus himself came to bring life, not death. In John 10:10, Jesus said, "The thief does not come except to steal, and to kill, and to destroy. I have come that they may have life, and that they may have it more abundantly." Jesus brings life, but if you look at the issues or platform of far-left politicians, it is plain to see that it leads to death and destruction. It doesn't lead to life.

Some people don't want to hear the truth. And when people have a problem with the truth, you can lie to them all day long and they'll eat it up. Some people hate the truth, but the truth is the only thing that will set us free. Those who stand against God by supporting all types of corruption that lead people down the highway to hell are enemies of God who need to repent of their sins in order to avoid everlasting torment.

In John 14:15, Jesus said, "If you love Me, keep My commandments." The Bible also says, "The fear of the Lord is the beginning of wisdom" (Proverbs 9:10). Some of these corrupt politicians have proven time and time again that they have not even begun to have an ounce of wisdom because they have no love and no fear of God or his commandments. They don't respect God, and the policies and laws they create prove it. Likewise, when you do not respect or reverence God by supporting politicians who have no reverence or fear for the laws of God, you, your family, and your community will pay the price for the decisions you make.

Psalm 25:12-14 says, "Who is the man that fears the Lord? Him shall He teach in the way He chooses. He himself shall dwell in prosperity, and his descendants shall inherit the earth. The secret of the Lord is with those who fear Him, and He will show them His covenant."

Quite frankly, a lot of blacks in America are not prospering or coming out of bondage, and they are not able to pass on an inheritance to the next generation, because they simply do not fear or respect God enough. They have worshiped their racial grievances and they have worshipped their culture and color above Christ. They're worshiping the system; worshiping a political party more than they worship God. They're looking for men to bring them out, and looking for politicians to bring them out, instead of God's kind of leadership. They're not fearing God; therefore, they're not dwelling in prosperity as mentioned in Psalm 25. They're staying in poverty and not passing an inheritance on to their descendants. The Psalm also says, "The secret of the Lord is with those who fear Him," meaning those who respect and reverence God. How can you respect and reverence God if you vote for and support a party that clearly stands for perversion, death, and everything else God is against? We are not supposed to make a religion out of any political party—Democrat or Republican. We are not supposed to follow either of these parties in a blind fashion. Our number one loyalty should be to God above, but unfortunately a lot of black people—and white people for that matter—have been more loyal to their political party than to God. So whose side are you on? Are you on the side of the Lord, or are you on the side of the ungodly political leaders?

Some Democrats love to accuse all Republicans of being racists in order to stir up fear to get the blacks to vote only for Democrats. We know for a fact that there are some white racists in America, but it is not fair to classify all whites as racists—or to classify all Republicans as racists—when in actuality the Democrat policies prove that they are the biggest racists. As long as there is sin in the world, there will be some racism in every part of the world. So we should hate the sin of racism, but we should not hate people or overreact to racism. And it is not sensible to destroy an entire community through rioting and violence just because there are some racists in the world. So if you are one of those blacks who will not take responsibility and will try to blame America or blame the white man for everything bad in the world, you will not make it into your Promised Land—you will die in the wilderness if you do not repent of this attitude of hate and unforgiveness. The Promised Land is not for the black Americans who grumble and complain and falsely blame.

Remember, even under the leadership of Moses, there were many Israelites who did not make it to the Promised Land because of their disobedience. In Exodus 32:26, Moses was dealing with rebellion in the camp and said, "Whoever is on the Lord's side—come to me!" When another rebellion took place in Numbers 16:32, the ground opened up and swallowed those Israelites who were not on the Lord's side—they were destroyed because they rebelled against the Lord and Moses, God's chosen leader. Those black people who are out in the street rebelling against God and government authorities, rioting, and doing other destructive things will not make it into the Promised Land or receive God's blessings. If they do not repent of their destructive, lawless, and hateful deeds, they can eventually be destroyed in the wilderness.

In Numbers 16:26, Moses told the people who were on the Lord's side to get away from the rebels: "And he spoke to the congregation, saying, 'Depart now from the tents of these wicked men! Touch nothing of theirs, lest you be consumed in all their sins.'" In reference to this incident with a rebel named Korah, the Bible lets us know that those who were not on the Lord's side were destroyed when the ground swallowed up many people, and thousands more were destroyed by a plague that suddenly came upon the land as judgment against the rebels: "Now those who died in the plague were fourteen thousand seven hundred, besides those who died in the Korah incident," it says in Numbers 16:49.

In a day and time like this where our entire world is faced with the coronavirus plague, this is no time to be rioting and rebelling against God, disrespecting authorities, playing religion, or playing with God. These are serious times, and in order to avoid destruction, it is time to get right with God, rather than mock God. Those white and black people who are rebelling and rioting in the streets are making things worse for America as a whole, and are especially making it worse for poor black Americans; so you need to separate yourself completely from these rebels if you are on the Lord's side. This is no time for being wishy-washy; this is the time to choose life over destruction and death. It is time to get on the Lord's side and to totally reject the far-left liberal politicians and their destructive ideologies.

I want to make it clear that I believe this is the season that a positive change will come for many in black America; but it is primarily for those black Americans who will not sell out to corrupt politicians but will obey the laws of God. Those who do not fear God will not make it into the "Promised Land." The blacks who decide to stay on the plantation with the blind leaders of the blind will not truly prosper. Even if they somehow get their hands on lots of money as pro athletes or by some other means, they will risk losing it by not fearing God, and they will invite all types of destruction into their lives and into their families, because reaping and sowing will always come into play whenever God's laws are mocked.

To bring out this point, Numbers 16:32 says, "and the earth opened its mouth and swallowed them up, with their households and all the men with Korah, with all their goods"—letting us know that when people rebel against God, they can lose their material possessions, their lives, and their households or families as well. But for those blacks who will respect God and reject corrupt politicians with ungodly values, they will set themselves up to truly prosper and enter into a whole new season of goodness and mercy for the rest of their lives. When I reverence God, the Bible lets me know that "Surely goodness and mercy shall follow me all the days of my life: and I will dwell in the house of the Lord for ever" (Psalm 23:6 KJV).

Black Americans must stop selling out just to get handouts from the politicians. Don't sell your soul just to get a few crumbs or a little bit of free stuff. God can give you much more than the politicians ever will. And a lot of black preachers and pastors should be especially ashamed and should really repent for selling out and giving support to a political party just because they gave a false promise of social justice, along with giving a few bread crumbs. These pastors are teaching their congregations to trust in a political party more than God. How can a political party offer black people true social justice when they support so much corruption and don't even respect the righteous and just laws of God?

Pastors should be teaching their congregations not to support politicians that embrace a multitude of corrupt policies that are totally contrary to God's laws. I am especially talking to black preachers and black people in general in this chapter, but regardless of your race or color, if you are a true believer in God's uncompromising truth, you need to say: "I refuse to support ungodly politicians because I am on the Lord's side."

Even if you are not crazy about the Republican Party and feel that they don't do enough to reach out to the black community, you have to admit that their policies do not blatantly defy the laws of God, and many of the conservative policies actually support noble virtues like faith, family values, life, traditional marriage, free enterprise, religious freedom, etc.

In other words, voting for conservative candidates will give you much greater freedom and opportunities to live for the Lord and prosper without government interference or oppression; whereas far-left liberal politicians have a track record of trying to bully, oppress, and sue those who truly want to follow God's laws. But many blacks who have been brainwashed by far-left politicians falsely believe that all Republicans are racists who will stop them from getting the social justice or the government handouts they deserve.

The truth is, there are some prejudiced people in the Republican Party and in the Democratic Party because sinners are everywhere; and when I vote I know it is not realistic to expect either party to have nothing but saints in it. But in reality, the lawless policies of the far-left liberal politicians are actually hindering true social justice and are destroying the black community the most. So I choose to be on the side of the conservative politicians who have the platform, policies, and values that are much more in line with my biblical values.

Those on the far-left are also big supporters of abortion, and the majority of babies being aborted are black babies; that's annihilation. And the fact is blacks can't even see that many of the politicians they vote for are standing for the annihilation of black Americans, but yet they are still voting for them and they are still following them. And even a lot of people who claim to be Christians actually stand for abortion.

A true Christian should realize that when you are stand-ing for abortion you are standing against one of the Ten Commandments—thou shall not kill. So how can you claim to be a true child of God and stand against the Word of God? Exodus 31:18 says the Ten Commandments were "written with the finger of God." And the Bible teaches us in Matthew 5:17 that Jesus did not deny the commandments, because he said he came to fulfill the law and not to abolish it.

In Matthew 22:34-40, Jesus also said, "'You shall love the Lord your God with all your heart, with all your soul, and with all your mind.' This is the first and great commandment. And the second is like it: 'You shall love your neighbor as yourself.' On these two commandments hang all the Law and the Prophets."

Kanye West is a well-known celebrity who has decided that he will not give blind support to any political party. At one of his 2019 Gospel events referred to as a "Sunday Service" session, West made a bold statement in defense of his support of President Trump, stating, "You black, so you can't like Trump? I ain't never made a decision only based on my color. That's a form of slavery, mental slavery."[1] West brought out the truthful point that it is "mental slavery" to make decisions or vote based on skin color. During a May 2019 talk show interview with David Letterman, West also stated that "Liberals bully people who are Trump supporters."[2]

Kanye West also drew controversy when he met Republican President Donald Trump at the White House in 2018, and at his 2019 Sunday Service event he also told the congregation that it was the Republican Party that freed the black slaves.[3] Most importantly, in an October 2019 interview, West credited his faith in Jesus Christ as the thing that set him free from the clutches of the Democratic Party. He also said the Democratic Party has backed policies for decades that have hurt the black community and have brainwashed blacks to do unholy things like encouraging the abortion of babies. "Thou shall not kill," West stated.[4]

Regardless of what you think about Kanye West, if you are a fair-minded human being who knows the facts, you have to admit that he is speaking truth about these controversial political issues. In his October 2019 interview, West also argued that it is very racist for someone to tell him that he is supposed to choose something based on his race. In the interview, he also pointed out that black people have been "brainwashed" by Democrats in America and that they "had us voting Democrats for food stamps for years, bro." He added, "The most racist thing a person could tell me is that I'm supposed to choose something based on my race." In reference to his parents who participated in the civil rights movement, West said, "they were fighting for us to have the right to our opinion, not the right to vote for whoever the white liberals said black people are supposed to vote for."[5]

Just like Kanye West has decided he will not blindly follow any political party, what decision will you make? Whatever choice you make, you must ultimately choose to be on the side of the Lord.

CHAPTER 5

DO YOU WORSHIP
COLOR OR CHRIST?

One of the main reasons so many blacks blindly support far-left politicians is because a lot of black people are prejudiced and are taught not to trust white people—unless they are white Democrats. So blacks allow politicians to constantly use the race card to persuade them to fight against some of the good Republican candidates, while supporting some of the ungodly liberals who pretend to offer racial equality but actually stand for nothing. This is foolish racism coming from a lot of black people, and this racism has kept a lot of blacks in ignorance and bondage.

The problem is that too many black people are worshiping their ethnicity or color more than worshiping Christ. If our power was in our color, our culture, or nationality, then we would have never been in slavery. Our deliverance is not in our racial or ethnic identity, it's in God. And black people as a race of people must look to God to be the deliverer. Too many people in the black community have looked to man and have looked to politicians who have done nothing for them. Man's power cannot deliver. It takes God to deliver any community of people out of bondage and oppression.

We've looked to man for years and we have failed because our trust was in man, and Proverbs 3:5-6 says, "Trust in the Lord with all your heart, and lean not on your own understanding;

in all your ways acknowledge Him, and He shall direct your paths."

Many in the Christian community are not even looking to God. And many of the black pastors or ministers I know are racists themselves. And I know thousands of them. This might sound surprising to some, but a lot of black ministers are just as racist as they claim other races of people are. A lot of black people are prejudiced toward some other races—and especially toward the Caucasian—and they sit there and carry this facade as if racism is only in the white community.

The root cause of racism or prejudice is sin, and in the black community many of the adults haven't taught the children to love and forgive. They have taught them to hate and they have taught them to ostracize and demonize everybody that's not black; but that is not of God and that's not the message that's supposed to come from the pulpit. The pulpit message should be if you humble yourself, then God will fight your battle, because 1 Peter 5:6 says, "Humble yourselves therefore under the mighty hand of God, that he may exalt you in due time." But many preachers have not taught this message in the community. Instead, they influence their congregations to vote for unrighteous liberal politicians in order to get their free cheese and butter or other handouts from the government, and these preachers need to repent for this. This is trusting in man, not God.

Our steps are to be ordered by the Holy Scriptures, not by ungodly politicians. President Trump is a political leader who is standing for Christian values and liberties. And then for many in the church to not go along with him is sickening; it's pathetic—then they call themselves children of God. It is common knowledge that there are some white churches that are prejudiced towards black people, but it is also very sad to me that many of the black churches are also prejudiced. And they go out and call the whites racists, while many themselves are racists. I went to seminary with 270 pastors, and I know thousands of black preachers—and many are fighting this demonic hold from the past to not be prejudiced against white people, and they are finding it is still a battle. They may have a reason, but one thing about the love of God is that it will take racist mess out of anyone's spirit.

When I first asked God to send someone in authority to help the black community, the Lord had to rebuke the prejudice in me, to allow me to know that race doesn't matter. If you need help and you are drowning, you don't care what the rescue squad color may be. You don't care. If a boat is coming and you are drowning, you aren't going to ask that man who comes to rescue you, "Are you a Ku Klux Klan member?" No, you are not. If he pulls you out of that deep water where you were sinking, you don't care what his name is, you don't care what color his skin is, and you don't care what race he is. That's what the Lord had to show me. It doesn't matter who it is that helps you if God has sent them to you. If the Lord sends somebody to help you, you accept the help and give God praise. It's not about color.

God sent President Trump to be a great help to the black community, and we need to stop focusing on color and recognize the good things the President has already done for blacks in America. God also showed me that everybody that fights against President Trump will reap what they sow. They will fall in the ditch that they try to dig for him. They will be defeated or destroyed, because God put Donald Trump in the office of President. Just like they threatened to impeach him and were trying to get him out of office, look now how the Democrats are being exposed for all the dirty work they have done; because the ditch they dug for President Trump, they're falling in it now. They don't understand that the Word of God is going to be manifested, and nothing will change the Word of God. I knew that when they dug the ditch for him, they were going to fall in it. And I knew the stone they tried to roll on his head was coming back on theirs; and it's happening right now because the dirty things they were trying to do are now being exposed. Rather than fight those who are sent by God to help us, we need to get on God's bandwagon and acknowledge what God is doing. If we don't acknowledge God, then where will our help come from? Without God we'll never have the help or the power to bring ourselves out because we are in the minority. And we can never overcome giant obstacles unless it is done with God's power. This is similar to what the Jews had to do to be delivered from the Egyptians in the Bible. God has to send the deliverer and bring deliverance. You can't come out on your own through destructive riots and violence, because if you try, you will be destroyed.

Hebrews 13:8 says, "Jesus Christ is the same yesterday, today, and forever," and Malachi 3:6 says, "For I am the Lord, I do not change." This lets us know that God can bring black Americans out the same way he brought the Israelites out of servitude and bondage. The Bible also says, "Of a truth I perceive that God is no respecter of persons: but in every nation he that feareth him, and worketh righteousness, is accepted with him" (Acts 10:34-35 KJV). This lets us know that what he does for one he will do for another, regardless of nationality or ethnicity. And because God is no respecter of persons, then what is required for one will be required for the other; so black people in America need to cry out to the Lord the same way the Israelites had to repent and cry out to God for deliverance.

Therefore, we have no other chance to come out of servitude except through Jesus Christ our Lord. We have to seek the face of God and be obedient to God in order to get his attention and compassion to lead us out; because trying to come out on your own is not going to work.

Any person supporting rioting or other types of ungodly activities has been deceived, because the Word of God teaches us in 1 John 4:20-21 that we know we love God when we love our brothers and sisters: "If someone says, 'I love God,' and hates his brother, he is a liar; for he who does not love his brother whom he has seen, how can he love God whom he has not seen? And this commandment we have from Him: that he who loves God must love his brother also."

When we have love for our brothers and sisters, that's how we know we've been born again; so if you have no love for your neighbors, no love for the next person, no love for the individual that you walk with or live with, or see every day, if you have no love for them, how can you claim to know God? The people who are rioting in the streets and rebelling against the police are destructive, and nobody should agree with this type of worldly destruction. This is demonic worldliness. This is activity of the devil himself that comes to steal, kill, and destroy. This is nothing but playing havoc in the streets. It is not spiritually right and nobody should put the good Lord's name on any of it. It is the spirit of the antichrist, and everybody involved in it is influenced by the antichrist spirit.

The Bible warns us not to be partakers of other people's sins, so Christians should have nothing to do with these types of destructive activities or with organizations that promote destruction. We are either with God or we are against him. You can't be on both sides. You need to make up your mind. For Christ I live and for Christ I die. You are not supposed to choose what feels right in the sight of man. It's not going to get you anywhere. The Black Lives Matter movement will not set people free. Except God delivers a people, they will never be free. Slavery was abolished in 1865, but black people have been in bondage and servitude since then. There is no real deliverance without God.

Improving race relations in America won't be done by people who riot and take the law into their own hands—trying to fix what only God can fix. What good does it do to bully somebody into recognizing you as a black person, but in their heart, they still hate you? God is the only one that can change things in the heart of man. If a person discriminates against you and you go against them, that won't change that person's heart. They will just go underground with their prejudice or racism. It's only the love of God that truly transforms people. You've got to do it God's way.

You can't fight hate with hate, with bullying, and with force. It doesn't mean a person's heart is going to change just because you try to force a person to act a certain way. It doesn't mean they are not prejudiced. All it's going to do is make people hide racism. And that's harder on black people when racism is in the heart but it's not shown, because you don't know who you're dealing with when it goes underground. These black people who are acting up in the streets don't understand that they are making the real racists even more angry, and they could retaliate. What they're doing is digging a pit for their own people to fall in. They are making race relations worse in America. And it will take God to bring us out of this mess.

I also would like to make a plea for peace between the black community and law enforcement in general. We as children of God, along with ministers and other community leaders, must demonstrate and teach the love of God in every situation. We should all consider each other as God would have us to, and we should try to imagine walking in the shoes of another.

In Matthew 7:12, Jesus said, "Therefore, whatever you want men to do to you, do also to them, for this is the Law and the Prophets." This simply means we should treat others the way we would want to be treated.

In John 13:34, Jesus also said, "A new commandment I give to you, that you love one another; as I have loved you, that you also love one another." We should always seek love and peace in every situation.

If people in general would try to imagine walking in the shoes of a police officer during these dangerous times, perhaps we would have more cooperation and respect for law enforcement. The anarchy in the streets seems to have contributed to some of the recent events in which police officers have killed black men. Unfortunately, this anarchy is sending a message that black men should not respect the police. And there are times when some police officers are afraid for their lives because of this lack of respect they are getting. Consequently, some officers overreact during an altercation because they fear that a black man will shoot them at the drop of a hat.

Furthermore, the disrespectful attitude of some of the black men in the streets causes them to resist arrest, which has led to some of them getting shot. Black males and others should always be taught to respect officers of the law—knowing that if they resist arrest or ignore orders from the police, there are repercussions that can follow. These police officers have families and children too, and they want to come home to their families. We must all try to see it from their side, even if we do not have family members in law enforcement.

Many people are also brainwashed by lying liberal news networks that are putting law enforcement in general in a negative light. President Trump is right by referring to what they put out as fake news. These networks are also part of the liberal propaganda machine and will rarely report anything favorable about President Trump or Republicans in general. I personally recommend that you watch programs like The 700 Club or watch someone like Sean Hannity on Fox News in order to find out what's going on in our world in a more truthful way. You also need to be careful what programs you watch on any of the news networks, because a number of liberal viewpoints—along with some racially insensitive perspectives—are propagated on some networks at times. So you obviously cannot just believe everything you hear on the news. But I would still choose certain programs on Fox News over the far-left liberal networks on any day, because at least Fox News does put forth the effort to be fair and balanced. But the far-left liberal media in general will brainwash you a whole lot more and lead you into lawlessness if you allow it. Those of us who stand for truth must speak out against corruption. It's time to stop worshiping color over Christ! These liberal media channels are very biased, and they claim to be on the side of blacks, but they are actually the real racists.

Some of the newscasters who hate President Trump just hate him because he's helping blacks, and they don't want him to get credit for it. They're working against him because he is standing up for Judeo-Christian values. He stands for what's right, and he stands for the little man who can't speak for himself. They hate him because he's doing things that the Democrats have never done. Had the Democrats done these things, blacks wouldn't be in the same hell hole they have been in for generations. But many don't just hate President Trump; they hate the God in him. And in many cases, it shows that they really don't truly care about African Americans and how much Donald Trump is helping them.

Members of the mainstream news media do not list how many black children and black young men are killed every day in our streets. They don't list anything or give any notoriety to the worst problems in the black community. And that's proof that they don't really care about blacks and that they are against blacks; but they are hiding it through their media coverage because of the lying, antichrist spirit that is operating through liberal media. If they really cared for blacks, then they would highlight the things that help the black community. They are the real enemies of black people.

If you are on the Lord's side, you need to stop listening to these corrupt people on television. They are devils in disguise, and they are used by Satan. But they don't realize that their tongues are cursed, because they will reap what they sow when they speak vicious lies and words of accusation against God's children. The Bible says, "No weapon that is formed against you will prosper; and every tongue that accuses you in judgment you will condemn. This is the heritage of the servants of the Lord, and their vindication is from Me," declares the Lord (Isaiah 54:17 NASB).

Their ratings are dropping, showing that they are not in favor with God. God is not the author of confusion and that's what the whole liberal media coverage is—it's confusion. They tell lies, and they propagate stuff that's not true, and they don't take the time to verify whether or not it's true. But they will report on every negative thing they can come up with, because they are full of confusion. They are being used by an antichrist spirit and the devil is their author; and if they don't get straight, they are going to deal with God, because the word of God says, "Do not be deceived, God is not mocked; for whatever a man sows, that he will also reap" (Galatians 6:7).

Just like I said before, if they dig a ditch for President Trump, they're going to fall in it first, and if they roll a stone to try to get it on his head, it's coming back on theirs. God's Word doesn't lie. That's why some of the politicians who tried to impeach President Trump are now under investigation. Now the same stone they tried to roll on his head is coming back on their heads. Now they're having to answer to the Senate for all the lawless things they have done. That's why whatever a man sows, he will reap, whether it's good or bad. If people understood that, then they would be careful how they treat one another. That's why I always taught my children to do unto others as you would have others do unto you, like Jesus taught in Matthew 7:12. I always teach people not to mistreat anybody. I don't care who it is, whether it's a homeless person or a person begging for money on the street. When you do unjust or mean things to others, it can come back on you.

If you are a black Christian person who has been brainwashed by liberal media to vote for a corrupt candidate just because they are a black Democrat or a white Democrat who makes false promises and gives false hope to blacks, then your identity is too much into your blackness as opposed to who you are in Christ. I especially want to ask blacks who claim to be Christians: do you worship your color or do you worship Christ?

Unfortunately, many liberal politicians have deceived blacks with the race card—and these politicians make millions of dollars with race-baiting tactics. They know that a lot of black people have been deeply wounded by racism, so politicians use this to stir up angry emotions in black people to the point that many blacks have even contradicted their Christian values just to support the political party that claims to stand for racial equality.

I am appealing to blacks in America and asking you to stop letting a political party brainwash you with the race card. Just because they lie to you and promise to free you from racism and discrimination and white oppression, you sell out to them and empower them to make this country more and more ungodly with their corrupt policies. Black people—including black preachers—you must stop worshiping your color more than you worship Christ.

CHAPTER 6

NEVER TRUMPERS, HATERS, AND TRAITORS

The level of undeserved hatred and criticism President Trump receives is astounding. When I started to share my prophetic vision about Donald Trump, a lot of black ministers got mad at me. When I told them Donald Trump is going to be president, they got upset with me and told me that God didn't show me that. I said, "We'll see," because I knew that time would tell the story and prove that God really showed me these things. But when I was sharing how God showed me that Donald Trump would become the next president and would also be used by God to help black Americans, some people would just get up and walk out of church during a revival meeting or at some other type of church event where we would be talking, testifying about voting and stuff like that. They would say, "Oh well, you know Trump's running' for president and he don't need to win; ya'll need to vote for Hillary."

And then they would say, "Oh well, you know the Democrats, they're the ones lookin' out for us." And I would say, "I've been praying and asking the Lord to send a leader who can help us, and the Lord showed me that Donald Trump is the one." So that's how a lot of people just got upset with me and my husband.

People would say, "I know you ain't votin' for no Donald Trump," and my husband would have to straighten them out a lot of times when they would get really upset and angry; because we would tell them God said Donald Trump was going to be president. As a matter of fact, when Donald Trump was running against Hillary, one of my brothers who is a pastor had a campaign event for Donald Trump and they shot his car up. They shot his SUV up. Thank God he wasn't in it. There are some black people who are really arrogant when it comes to anybody supporting President Trump, and the majority of them want to support ungodly politicians regardless of how much they claim to believe in God. But many of these people really don't know God. They don't know God and they're not asking the Lord who to vote for.

When the black preachers would tell me that Trump is a billionaire white man who doesn't care anything about black people, I would say to these preachers: "If you're in a hole and you're drowning and you're in the sea, and you don't have a life boat, do you ask the rescue squad or the person that's coming to help you, are you prejudiced and do you love black people? No, you would take the help that comes to you because you are in a life-and-death situation."

Furthermore, I said to those haters: "You all need to get some common sense and stop thinking about the color of people's skin and what you feel they are, and look at what they can do to help you." I also said: "Now during the Civil War when all those white Union Army Yankees from up North fought those white Confederate soldiers from the South so the black people could be freed from slavery, the black slaves didn't say 'Before I take help from those white Yankees I need to ask every Yankee are they prejudiced.' Nobody asked that because those white Yankees were down there putting their lives on the line and fighting a war to free blacks. It was a Civil War where the northern whites fought the southern whites for our liberty. If God decides to use anything or someone of any race to help us, why do you have a problem with it?"

Hundreds of thousands of men—mostly white—lost their lives to end slavery. Those black slaves did not allow themselves to be blinded by hate, so they were able to receive help from the white northerners. But today, a lot of people have blind hatred and don't want to receive help from a Republican president like Donald Trump. It is amazing to me that there were black and white Democrat politicians that hated President Trump so much that they tried to stop him from getting criminal justice reform done—even though a lot of black prisoners were eventually released from unjust prison sentences as a result of what President Trump accomplished through this bipartisan criminal justice reform bill.

This really demonstrates the level of deception and blind hatred that is coming from so many people on the far-left. Some of these politicians would rather see black prisoners suffer unjust prison sentences and rot in jail than work with President Donald Trump. It is the same level of blind hatred that causes far-left mayors or governors to refuse to let President Trump send them the National Guard or military help they need to stop their cities from getting burned down from all the violent protests and riots related to the death of George Floyd.

That's because there are a lot of politicians filled with blind hatred—and I even know black pastors who are deceived with blind hatred as well. When we had the credit union, for example, my husband and I put together a coalition of churches and we had hundreds of ministers and pastors in the coalition, and that was another way I knew and shared with many pastors the vision about Donald Trump becoming president. Many of these pastors and ministers all knew me as a community leader, but they really didn't like or believe my prophecy about Donald Trump being the next president. When we would have conferences or conventions throughout the country, I would talk to a lot of these pastors on the phone, Internet, and the whole nine yards. And when I would share with them about how God was going to put Donald Trump in the White House, basically they would say something like, "Oh well, I don't know about that," and they were holding things against him even though they didn't even know him. "Oh yeah, he ain't nothin' but an ol' rich man," they would say, and I would tell them, "A poor person can't do anything for you. How can a poor person help you?"

Unfortunately, there are even some liberal politicians who would rather see people die than give President Trump credit for anything good he did. On August 10, 2020, The 700 Club did a special report showing how a lot of the liberals are even discrediting a medication called hydroxychloroquine just because Donald Trump used it and recommended it.[1] The drug has been considered safe and effective for decades, and some very credible and qualified doctors have proven that it is a medication that can actually help overcome coronavirus—especially in its early stages. But the politically correct elite are kicking these doctors off of social media and claiming that the doctors are promoting a dangerous medication. The liberals are lying and keeping people from this source of potential help just because they hate Donald Trump!

Some very qualified doctors who spoke in favor of hydroxychloroquine got banned from social media platforms like Facebook, Google, YouTube, and Twitter. One of the doctors was even fired from her job at a hospital due to the backlash. What these liberals are doing is sinister, corrupt, ungodly—all for the greed of money and power. They will allow people to die and to be destroyed from COVID-19 and will deny people of medication that could help them—all because of hatred for the president and greed for power. This is twisted. Its more proof that far-left liberals will cause you to die if you follow them.

A recent news report that tells how the Democrats recently persecuted one of their own party members brings out this point further. In March of 2020, a black Democratic State Representative named Karen Whitsett of Detroit was infected with COVID-19, and she credited the hydroxychloroquine medication with saving her life. She also gave President Trump credit for using his influence to help make it available when many states were trying to ban it for political reasons. She even went to the White House on April 14, 2020, and personally thanked President Trump. "Thank you for everything that you have done," she told President Trump at the meeting.[2] But because she is a member of the Democratic Party, she received backlash from many of the Democrat leaders who wanted to punish her just for saying something good about President Trump. Her angry 13th Congressional District Democratic Party Organization decided to vote on a resolution related to denying her their future endorsement and banning her from their activities for the next two election cycles. Those Democratic leaders basically made her an outcast just because she publicly thanked President Trump for making it possible for her to get a medication that saved her life. "If President Trump had not talked about this, it wouldn't have been something that would be accessible for anyone to be able to get right now," Karen Whitsett said.[3] When she was also asked whether she thinks President Trump may have saved her life, Whitsett said: "Yes, I do," and "I do thank him for that."[4]

Georgia Democratic State Representative Vernon Jones is another black Democrat who got a taste of the blind hatred from his own party. The Democratic Georgia representative resigned from his office because of backlash he received after he endorsed President Trump for reelection. Jones came under heavy attack and his own party planned to punish him because he said positive things about Donald Trump.

Jones, after his original endorsement, told the Journal-Constitution newspaper that "President Trump's handling of the economy, his support for historically black colleges, and his criminal justice initiatives drew me to endorse his campaign."[5]

In April 2020, Jones tweeted: "I've seen more Democrats attack me for my decision to endorse @realdonaldtrump than ask me why," he said. "They've used and abused folks in my community for far too long, taking our votes for granted. Black Americans are waking up. An uprising is near."

After he announced his resignation, Jones fired off tweets that showed support for Trump and disdain for Democrats. He tweeted: "More African-Americans, prior to this pandemic, were working more than any other time in my lifetime" and also said that "[t]he left hates me because they can't control me. They can stay mad."

In the statement announcing his resignation, Jones also told the Journal-Constitution: "I intend to help the Democrat Party get rid of its bigotry against black people that are independent and conservative. I endorsed the white guy (Donald J. Trump) that let blacks out of jail, and they endorsed the white guy (Joe Biden) that put blacks in jail."[6]

Kevin O'Leary experienced division with family members of his own household because of disagreements about President Trump. Many people know Kevin O'Leary as the famous multimillionaire businessman, investor, and personality from the Shark Tank reality TV show. O'Leary, who is liberal on many social issues—but against socialism—is a successful businessman who gives President Trump a lot of credit for getting rid of a lot of hindering business regulations or rules that were making it very hard for a lot of American businesses to prosper.

In a 2019 interview, O'Leary made it plain that when it comes to Trump, he focuses more on the substance rather than the personality, and this is what he said regarding how much President Trump's policies have helped our economy: "My take on Trump and his cabinet . . . I look at the policy. . . . I have interest in . . . over fifty private companies now in practically every state. . . . I have never in my life seen an economy like this. This is even better than the sixties. It is phenomenal, and I think primarily because of deregulation, not tax reform. My companies in California, in Texas, in Florida, in Illinois, at the municipal level and the state level, have been set free."[7]

O'Leary further pointed out how there were all kinds of absurd regulations on the books since the fifties, but "Trump swept all that garbage away. . . . All of a sudden, I can open up stores all across California where I never could. Just like that."[8]

The host who interviewed O'Leary was obviously not a fan of Trump, and he asked O'Leary if Trump's extremely divisive, racist rhetoric bothers him.

"I met Trump," O'Leary said, [and] in many ways his style is difficult. . . . I don't believe he's a racist man. I don't believe that at all. I don't think he's a sexist man, I don't believe that at all. . . . I think he's a family man, but people don't get that."

O'Leary also brought out the point that the Donald Trump presidency even caused some division in his family because, on the night Trump got elected, O'Leary said his daughter was so discouraged that she wept. And O'Leary said to his daughter, "This is a really good thing that just happened; you just don't know it yet."[9]

O'Leary says he keeps trying to sell some of his own family members on the merits of Trump's policies, but he realizes that some of their opinions will not change, and this reflects the division in America as a whole.

Why are there so many "Never Trumpers," haters, and traitors when it comes to President Donald Trump? (The Never Trumpers are the so-called conservatives or Republicans who hate Donald Trump to the point that some of them have even pledged their support to vote for the Democratic presidential candidate.) President Trump has probably had more people despise him, turn on him, and betray him than any president in the history of this country. He has probably been called a racist more times than any president before him. His own niece wrote a negative book about him. Many people who once served in his cabinet left and said all types of nasty things about him. One reason he is hated so much is because there is nothing about Donald Trump that is politically correct. That is one reason why the people who hate him hate him so much, and a reason why the people who love him love him so much. There's nothing about him that buckles down to political correctness. He boldly goes against the grain of corrupt systems and corrupt people, and this is what he means when he says he is "draining the swamp."

Even ex-NFL running back Herschel Walker says he's lost friends because of his support for Donald Trump. Herschel recently spoke during the Republican National Convention on August 24, 2020, and explained that Donald Trump never asked him to speak for him. But this outstanding black athlete decided to do the speech of his own free will because he was tired of hearing people say so many untrue things about President Donald Trump.

In his speech, the former Heisman trophy winner explained that he has had a deep personal friendship with Donald Trump for 37 years. "It hurt my soul to hear the terrible names that people call Donald," he said. "The worst one is racist. I take it as a personal insult that people would think I've had a 37-year friendship with a racist. People who think that don't know what they're talking about. Growing up in the deep South, I've seen racism up close. I know what it is, and it isn't Donald Trump."[10] In his speech, Herschel also stated that President Trump's actions speak louder than stickers or slogans on a jersey, because Donald Trump shows how much he cares about social justice in the black community through his actions.

In an interview with Laura Ingraham on Fox News, Walker said, "Donald Trump has done more in three years than . . .

most presidents have done in eight, and what's so special about him is he cares about people. . . .This president here has done almost everything he said that he was going to do and that counts."[11]

The former Georgia Bulldog running back also expressed his commitment to God, family, and country in a powerful way, saying: "First of all, I believe in God, I believe in family, I believe in the American flag, I believe in the national anthem. I believe in law and order. While the Democrat Party has not said that they believe in any of those things. That's what made America beautiful."[12]

Thank God for independent thinkers like Herschel Walker who refuse to be negatively influenced by the Never Trumpers, haters, and traitors in our world. Lord knows we need more sensible men like Herschel who refuse to put color above Christ. Not only was Herschel an unstoppable warrior on the football field, but it is good to see that he is a warrior for the Lord. My prayer is that everyone who reads this book will be inspired and emboldened to stand for what is right regardless of what the haters or traitors will try to do or say, because Romans 8:31 says, "If God is for us, who can be against us?"

CHAPTER 7

WHO WILL STAND IN THE MIDST OF THE LEADERSHIP CRISIS?

To me, the national anthem protests by NFL players at the football games seem to symbolize the wrong direction that a lot of people are going in our country. The way those athletes refuse to stand to salute the American flag is the same way many in our culture are refusing to stand for the Lord. There are some people who feel that bowing for the national anthem as a form of protest is not a bad idea, but I personally feel it is a slap in the face of all the people who believe in honoring God and country by standing and saluting the flag. The flag of the United States of America represents our patriotism and our Judeo-Christian values, and anyone who doesn't want to show respect during the national anthem is disrespecting that heritage as far as I'm concerned. So the question is: where are the leaders and people in general who will stand for the heritage and values that made this country great? Are the owners of all the pro sports leagues missing in action? Where are the owners who will say "I do not support anyone disrespecting our national anthem"?

America was started as a God-fearing and righteous nation by Christian people who respected God. Although the far-left liberals are trying to cover up our religious history and heritage, this country was founded by Christians. This nation was formed by God, and our founding fathers intended it to be a nation that would honor and respect God. Anybody who will disrespect a nation and a flag that was dedicated to Christ is influenced by the wrong spirit, and a lot of fans just don't want this type of thing going on at a sporting event.

Some of these individuals who kneel during the national anthem don't just disrespect this country, they also disrespect God and they are showing it by the disrespect to this nation—one of the only nations in the world that befriends Israel. The nation in the world that has promoted the Gospel of Jesus Christ more than all the other nations is the United States. And if they had any kind of respect for God and any kind of loyalty to Jesus Christ, they would pick up that cross and follow him. And when they would pick up that cross, they would honor this nation because of the God who formed this nation.

Because they kneel, they are disrespecting this nation, because by doing that they are disrespecting or dishonoring the flag that represents the United States of America. And anybody who goes against a God-fearing nation and works towards making it an antichrist nation is doing the work of the devil. They are the sons and daughters of the devil, and they are being used by Satan. And if they don't repent, the work they do against this nation is going to cause them to reap what they sow. Also, the owners and other leaders in the league who will allow all this protesting to go on will pay for it as well. Will any of these NFL executives or owners ever have the courage to stand against this disrespectful behavior in the midst of our politically correct culture?

Outspoken black American sportswriter and television host Jason Whitlock believes in solving the national anthem protest controversies with common sense. Whitlock understands that for years the game of football has been attached to patriotism, so having players protest during the national anthem is bad for business and it is also ineffective.

In a 2018 Fox Sports broadcast, Whitlock stated that the cure for toxic stupidity is common sense. As an example, Whitlock cited a controversy from 1996 when Denver Nuggets guard Mahmoud Abdul-Rauf publicly stated that the national anthem was a symbol of tyranny and oppression. Consequently, he decided he would not stand for the national anthem during NBA games. Whitlock explained how the NBA suspended Mahmoud Abdul-Rauf until he agreed to stand, and that quickly ended the protests and solved the problem.[1]

Whitlock says the NFL should impose a similar solution: if a player protests during the national anthem, that player is immediately suspended and fined. That's how you end this controversy. Thank God for the voice of common sense from Jason Whitlock. But unfortunately, the NFL did not use common sense and has allowed the players to get out of hand with protests.

More recently, while being interviewed by Tucker Carlson on Fox News in July 2020, Whitlock made some bold statements about the lack of leadership that allows these controversial protests to spread throughout the league. Whitlock pointed out how the NFL is unwise in letting players protest by bowing during the national anthem, while also allowing players to promote the Black Lives Matter movement at these sporting events. Whitlock believes the NFL could lose a large portion of its audience if they continue to have a failure of leadership. Whitlock further stated that there is no way anyone can do any research on Black Lives Matter and not see that it is a Marxist or Communist political organization that is not about black people. Whitlock also expressed his sheer disappointment for those people who claim to have religious values and claim to be Christians while sitting back and doing nothing to stand against these negative influences. In reference to these

Christians, Whitlock says, "This is a historic failure of men and leadership. This is cowardice at its highest level."[2] Whitlock also says the NFL in general no longer stands for the values they said they stood for, and he singles out NFL Commissioner Roger Goodell and all the team owners for not taking a stand. "This is NFL ownership," Whitlock said. "All of them. Cowards. Not standing up for what they believe in. America has made them filthy rich and some of the most powerful people on the planet, and they're unwilling to defend the values they built their business on, and the country that has enriched them incredibly . . . across the board . . . politically, in the sports world, I'm looking at men fall out of cowardice. I'm looking at women fall out of cowardice. It's pervasive throughout this country."[3]

Jason Whitlock hit the nail right on the head. Who will stand for what is right, and when will those who even call themselves Christians stop cowering in the corner? When we look at the state of the leadership in our nation, it reminds us all the more that we need a strong president like Donald J. Trump. It reminds us all the more that there is a crisis of leadership, and one reason President Trump gets so much opposition is because he has the guts to stand while so many others are just acting like politically correct cowards.

Some of these athletes, on the other hand, feel that by protesting this way they are bringing out the point that America has been a hypocritical nation that has enslaved and brutalized blacks. But these athletes fail to realize that there were demonic people in this country who misrepresented God by oppressing people, and these devilish people had nothing to do with our American forefathers and ancestors who created laws that honor God, and they also sacrificed their lives to set the slaves free. Like every nation, America has had dark moments, but it has also had many bright moments that outshine the darkness. A country is similar to a family from the standpoint that you cannot hate or dishonor your entire family because of the jailbirds or black sheep in the family who have done shameful things.

When you consider history, God's people—the Israelites—were in bondage like black people in America. There was a reason why the Israelites were in bondage. African Americans were in bondage and there was a reason they were in bondage. Everything happens for a reason. This does not justify the slave owners, but everything happens for a reason. And we should remember the past so as not to repeat it, but we cannot live in the past. You can't do anything about what happened to African Americans in the past. Neither can we do anything about what happened to the Israelites. But it is a privilege that God allowed us as African Americans to walk in a similar path as the Israelites, so we can line up with God's Word and focus on where we are going instead of where we have been.

When you look at the black athletes who made it out, they have received a lot of good fortune that many other blacks didn't get. And for those athletes to refuse to stand during the anthem and not be grateful to God for what the Lord has done for them is very unwise. With all the suffering that blacks in general have experienced, these rich black athletes should recognize that they have been crowned with loving-kindness and given favor to be in a sports league that was once for whites only. Now they get the opportunity to play in these sports leagues and pull down the kind of money that most people only dream about. These wealthy athletes should not show a lack of gratitude for the country that made them extremely successful.

These athletes owe God praise more than any of the other black people that are still in servitude and suffering and bondage. They made it out, so the least they can do is give God praise. They got a privilege and a favor that other blacks didn't get. And for them to disrespect God on that level, they're going to pay double in terms of negative consequences if they don't repent. They have an advantage that people their whole life work for and cry and pray for and don't get. Look at how many young men tried out for those leagues and didn't get on NFL and NBA teams. And for them to get that privilege and to throw it in God's face like they made it on their own; I say to them, "No, you didn't. People died for you to get where you're at. And you choose to disrespect the God that made you rich through the support of the fans you are disrespecting?" That's treacherous, because these athletes are not even thankful, and they forgot where they came from. And if you're not grateful for where you came from, guess what? You'll lose it. When you're not grateful for what God gave you, and you disrespect him and dishonor him by coming against the country that was started for his glory, you will pay the consequences. And every one of them that got rich is capable of losing those riches if they don't repent of their foolishness and show gratitude to the Lord.

A lot of sports fans are offended by these protests because many of the fans respect God, the country, and the flag. These athletes must understand that on any given day, millions of fans could decide they are not going to watch the games or buy tickets. What will these rich, arrogant athletes do then? They will be left with an empty stadium where they can protest all by themselves. They need to wise up and use their riches to make a difference in a more constructive way that does not offend so many fans. If they don't, they will lose everything, and then they won't be able to help a soul.

Any time you use your platform in a manner that does not respect God, you are behaving in an unlawful way. You are not acting in an honorable fashion. Romans 13:7 teaches us to give honor where honor is due. If you do not show proper honor to your country and the God who started it, you are not an individual who has deserved the honor you have received, and you will lose it. Every one of them who disrespects this country and the God who established it is setting themselves up to be losers.

The Word of God doesn't lie. Whatever the Word of God says will happen, will happen. Proverbs 16:18-19 says, "Pride goes before destruction, and a haughty spirit before a fall." And when they are arrogant enough to dishonor the flag, they are in danger of losing their professions. And you can tell them I said it. You don't disrespect God. Ever.

One thing about President Trump is that he respects God and the people of God; and he also stands for God with his principles and actions even louder than his words. Understandably, there are some who criticize the president for saying things in a rough way or for using a little profanity, like he did when he rebuked the NFL football players for bowing during the national anthem. But we must all remember that disciples have to be made and disciples have to grow. Remember how Peter cut off the ear of the soldier, and Jesus put it back on. Moses killed a man, yet he became God's chosen leader of the Israelites. Think about the Word of God and the things people have done. Paul killed Christians before he was converted, and he became the top apostle to help establish the New Testament church. Paul had a checkered past to the point that it took some of the Christians a while before they trusted him even after his conversion. Just because the Lord calls someone doesn't mean that person doesn't have a past. The point is that everybody has to grow in grace. And we all have sinned and come short of the glory of God, so we must be careful not be too nit-picky or self-righteous, and we must see the big picture of how God is using President Trump to help advance the kingdom of God. I believe President Trump is growing in the Lord. Nobody gets to be perfect overnight, and God is not through with Donald Trump yet. Neither is the Lord through with us.

President Trump is also hated by some people because he

never tries to be politically correct and he speaks his mind. A lot of black professional athletes got very angry at him when he told the NFL executives that they ought to fire the players who refuse to stand for the national anthem. Even though I am a black woman who has suffered and faced some discrimination in America myself, I love this country and I believe God is not pleased with the way these athletes are protesting. There is a time and place for all things, and what these athletes are doing is upsetting a lot of the fans who pay to see them play football—not protest.

In spite of the imperfections in our country, I believe those athletes should be respectful and show their gratitude to God and country by standing during the anthem. It was this country and the fans who come to the games who turned a lot of those athletes into millionaires, so they should be more respectful towards the way many fans feel about standing for the national anthem. Not only are these athletes giving off the impression that they are disrespecting the flag, the country, and God, but as previously mentioned, these athletes are also making a bad business decision because the customer is always right. They are making a bad spiritual decision and a bad business decision. Anybody in business should know that you do not disrespect your customers—the sports fans—and still expect to get paid. These men are cutting off the hands that feed them; they are being foolish and arrogant and will pay the price for it. The fans are not against the athletes hating police brutality, but the fans just don't want to see a protest at a sporting event that has nothing to do with police brutality. Just because there are bad cops out there does not mean that America is not a great nation, and it does not mean the athletes should disrespect the national anthem.

A lot of these athletes are using their influence to fight President Trump and to disrespect many of their fans by kneeling during the national anthem at sporting events, but I don't really see too many of them using their influence to help save these black communities from self-destruction. Shame on many of these arrogant, high-minded millionaire athletes. If they are not careful, they will drive many of their fans away and lose everything they have, because the fans are the ones who have made them rich. When it comes to not showing respect during the national anthem, a lot of fans view this as also disrespecting the flag and the people who died to make this country free. They see it as disrespectful to the hundreds of thousands of soldiers who even died during the Civil War to set the black slaves free. A lot of fans see bowing instead of standing during the national anthem as an act of disrespect to God, to the great men who started this nation on Judeo-Christian values, and to all the soldiers who died for the cause of freedom.

So these athletes should use some common sense and respect the wishes of the fans in general, because the fans are not asking them not to take a stand for justice; many of the fans just want to see the athletes stand just like everybody else during the national anthem. When you violate certain traditions and customs like these athletes are doing, you can pay a heavy price that is not worth it in the end. This is not a hard thing to figure out if you use some wisdom and common sense even from a business standpoint. There are a million and one ways these athletes can protest police brutality or use their celebrity status to make a difference; but they are very unwise in choosing a method of protest that offends many of the fans who made them rich and famous. To many of the fans, this is very disrespectful and foolish. And if these athletes do not come to their senses, they will pay a heavy price for it.

If these professional athletes do not come to this understanding, they will ruin themselves and the leagues they play in. And if the commissioners of these leagues do not have the courage to enforce rules during the national anthem, the sports leagues will pay a heavy price for it. Many of the fans are viewing these athletes as a bunch of arrogant, ungrateful souls who are disrespecting or even despising God and country. Their protests will backfire on them.

With issues like the coronavirus and all of the other natural disasters in the world that are already working against us, we do not need to work against ourselves by doing foolish things. And what these players are doing by biting off the hands that feed them is foolish. They care nothing about the millions of fans they are offending. Some of the sports leagues have already been shut down temporarily because of the coronavirus pandemic, so why would players want to risk losing more opportunities and more revenue by alienating fans with protests during the national anthem?

These are serious times and we all need to examine ourselves to make sure we are in line with God's will. We are living in a time when those who are not real for God will suffer most because the Lord is our only source of true hope with all the calamities taking place in the world.

And just because some of us are churchgoers, this alone does not save us. We need to truly know God and seek to obey him. Even many church doors have been closed because of the coronavirus plague, and this is a reminder of how much we all need God living inside of us instead of just going into a church building. The Bible lets us know that judgment starts at the house of God. And in these perilous times, it is time for people to stop just acting religious and to get serious about serving the Lord. 1 Peter 4:17 says "For the time has come for judgment to begin at the house of God; and if it begins with us first, what will be the end of those who do not obey the gospel of God?"

With all the disaster happening in our world, we should reverence God more than ever. This is no time for phoniness and foolishness. This is a time when we should be seeking to respect the authorities God places in our lives. This is no time to disrespect the police or the president for illegitimate reasons, because the Bible lets us know we are out of order when we disrespect the authority God has set before us. If people feared God more, they would not be so quick to tear down President Trump for any little reason. As I already said, it was unbelievable for me to see the number of black folks and even church leaders who opposed President Trump even when he was doing all the good things that God allowed him to do to help the church and Christians in America. Many of the people were so sin-sick, they would rather vote for a devil that has no idea what the truth is rather than support President Trump. Many of the preachers are so messed up and prejudiced, they get in the pulpit and talk against a man because of the color of his skin and because he is a Republican, not because of the message he's sending or the things he's doing.

A lot of these people have lost sight of God, and the Lord allowed me to see that he is not pleased with these things. The world is so wicked because not enough people are standing against sin, but instead a lot of people are introducing and endorsing sin—even a lot of pastors. This is why judgment has already started at the house of God. A lot of churches, whether they be white, Hispanic, black, or whatever, have made people's souls religious without true salvation, and some of these people are falling into hell. This is why so many people don't even know right from wrong when it comes to knowing who to vote for. A lot of so-called Christians have helped to put corrupt God-haters in office, and it is time for the church to repent of these things.

Thank the Lord that President Donald Trump is not a God-hater, but he hates political correctness because it is a danger to our nation. And politically correct people hate the God in President Donald Trump because God is using him as a wrecking ball against political correctness, and the Lord is also using him to help restore America back to its God-fearing heritage.

Therefore, he's hated by the forces of darkness. Democrats—and even some Republicans in his own party who want to play politics as usual—are against him. And even though Donald Trump has shown much favor to Christians and Jews, you even have some people who call themselves Christians who speak all manner of evil against this president and can't see any of the good he has done. Tell me that's not evil, ignorant, and demonic. He's helping to fight for the religious rights and liberties of Christians and Jews in a way that no other president has ever done before, and even some Christians fail to even acknowledge this.

Even though President Trump has proven that he will stand for the Judeo-Christian values that made this country great, I have still seen blind Christians who do not support this president that God has put in office because they don't like his tweets or because they feel he does not communicate in the most diplomatic or presidential manner. These Christians are not focusing on the big picture—we are in a war for this nation's soul. Some of these same judgmental, hypocritical Christians who are outraged because they feel Donald Trump said something in a blunt way are not looking at the overall good he is doing to protect the church from government oppression.

I also find it interesting and hypocritical that some of these same Christians who seem to be outraged at President Trump over matters related to his style are not outraged with the corrupt media or the liberal politicians who are trying to destroy this country with all types of immorality. And what about the corrupt politicians who have tried to crucify President Trump through an unjust and bogus impeachment process? President Trump's civil liberties were violated under the false pretense of Russian collusion using the FBI and CIA, and yet there are some Christians who will never pray for this president or appreciate how he has fought for the freedoms of Christians and Jews and Americans in general.

In only one term as president, Donald Trump has done an enormous amount of good, yet so many people—blacks, whites, Democrats, even many Republicans—are trying to work against him. This is why I know it is a vicious, demonic attack that is bringing forth an onslaught of lies and deception, because you cannot explain these things just from a natural standpoint. So many of the positive things the President has done often get overshadowed by the lies, the negative media coverage, and nasty things people say about him which are not true. But thank God President Trump has decided to stand in spite of all the hate and opposition, because God Almighty placed him where he is, and this satanic work will not affect him. But if it had been anyone else, the pressure alone would have been unbearable. Who do you know can live under this type of pressure and still get the job done, here and around the world, better and faster than anyone could have imagined?

In Luke 21:17, Jesus said, "And you will be hated by all for My name's sake," and in that same chapter Jesus also said you will be betrayed by relatives and friends. I believe this verse holds the key to explaining a lot of the persecution that President Trump has received. A lot of the policies the president supports benefit Christians and Jews—God's people who have been called out and chosen for His name's sake. This is why all hell has broken loose against this president, because he is standing for legislation and policies that can really stop the far-left government leaders from trying to silence and oppress God's people.

Consider also the words of Jesus from John 15:18-19: "If the world hates you, you know that it hated Me before it hated you. If you were of the world, the world would love its own. Yet because you are not of the world, but I chose you out of the world, therefore the world hates you." In verse 25, Jesus said it is written that "They hated Me without a cause."

Jesus referred to the devil as the father of lies and referred to those who live for the devil as his children. This is in John 8:44, when Jesus told the corrupt leaders of his day that "You are of your father the devil . . . for he is a liar and the father of it." The far-left liberal politicians and media personalities who have not repented of their sins are children of the devil, and they are spreading lies all the time about President Trump because this is their nature. This lets us know that when the father of lies blinds people with lies and deception, they will hate those who are doing right without a cause—the world will be against those who are not following in the footsteps of the world.

They don't just hate him; they hate the plan of God that is unfolding in him and through him. They hate him because on December 6, 2017, President Trump kept his promise and announced that the United States would begin recognizing Jerusalem as the capital of Israel. And on May 14, 2018, the United States officially opened our Embassy in Jerusalem. As a result of these actions, many people in the world hate him because he took a stand for Israel.

They hate him and accuse him of being a racist, because he is building a wall to protect our borders so that all types of corruption can no longer enter freely into our country, and to also stop drug trafficking that comes across the border and causes death in the black community. They hate when he stands up against abortion. They hate him when he stands up against all types of wickedness and corruption. They hate him when he makes a stand for Christianity and for true religious liberty so that the liberals can't try to bully God's people. They hate him when he stands up for the church. Will you also stand?

They hate President Trump when he stands up for black issues like criminal justice reform, because all these years these issues were never properly addressed until he started addressing them. He makes many of these haters—black and white—feel insecure because they did not have the guts to do what he has done. They were all talk, but he is a man of action. They hate him without a cause because he stands for what God wants. And any time you stand to please God, you will be hated of all men for His name's sake. Evil and corrupt people are trying to invent reasons to criticize this president every day, because they hate him without a cause. Because hateful people in high places hate President Trump without a cause, they create fake news and lies to misinform in order to cause other uninformed and ignorant people to hate him without a cause, so it is a vicious cycle of lies and deceit. But President Trump has the victory in spite of all this hate, because the Lord is on his side.

He is hated, and because he is hated, people think he has done something to be hated for. But he is hated because he is standing for righteousness. Anytime you stand to do right in a wrong world, anytime you stand to say what's right when so many others are thinking to do what's wrong, you will face opposition. They would've loved him if he would've agreed with abortion. If he would have been like the typical politician and would have agreed to allow blacks to stay in the rut that they're in, the political elite would be able to deal with him better because then he wouldn't remind them that they are full of failure, hypocrisy, and lies—all talk and no action.

President Trump is also hated by some because he has been putting the wall up to help stop murder and other crimes in our communities, and some of the black folks got out and said "oh he's puttin' the wall up 'cause he's prejudiced." I have been told by credible sources that these gangs are bringing drugs and guns into black communities, and many of these gang members came to this country illegally. In some cases, these foreign gang members place guns in our communities for all of these black boys to kill each other off so that the foreigners can take over the communities and replace black men.

While President Trump has been fighting to stop this

ruthless gang activity, a lot of people are constantly trying to work against him, accusing him of being a racist for having the common sense to build a wall. Unfortunately, a lot of these athletes who claim they are for social justice are too ignorant or mean-spirited to understand that one of the reasons the walls are being put up is to save blacks from the foreigners bringing guns and drugs into our communities and taking our jobs. These illegal aliens come over here and get on the payroll because they can work for less, and it has caused so many blacks to lose job opportunities. These are problems that most liberals never talk about because they want to blame everything on the police or on Donald Trump when we actually need the police—along with this law-and-order president—to help stop this gang activity.

Because President Trump cares about the safety of our communities, his administration has put a lot of resources into stopping the criminal activities of a notoriously brutal gang that was formed by illegal aliens from El Salvador, along with hundreds of thousands of others from Central America. A large share of these gang members are not U.S. citizens; so law enforcement agencies like U.S. Immigration and Customs Enforcement (ICE) would be much more effective at removing them from this country if the liberal politicians would stop protecting them through sanctuary cities.

While President Trump is trying to fight these liberal sanctuary cities in the U.S. that provide protection for the foreign gang members, he is facing all kinds of opposition from Americans who are falsely accusing him of being a racist when he is just trying to protect the black community and America as a whole from being taken over by these criminals.

This is why it grieves my spirit that certain famous black men—along with many others—are saying untrue things to tear down President Trump when this president is doing more for the black community than any other president has done.

When President Trump saw the destruction in the black community, he was outraged. He even told black politicians to go back to their cities to help the black children who are living in poverty with the roaches and rats running around. For years, the government has given a lot of money to cities like Chicago, Baltimore, and New York, but the black communities in these places still have slums and ghettos, all kinds of crime, and drug-infested areas. The children aren't safe even playing in front of their doors.

Donald Trump, God bless his heart, the Lord used him to stand up against the drug trafficking, against the drug activity. He stood up against the guns and ammunition coming into the community illegally—feeding our community with more murder and more dilapidation. Then he turned around and began to help create jobs with higher income for African Americans. He began to do prison reform to get some of these young men out of prison that the Democrats put in there with the "three strikes and you're out" rule; so that when some young man got three felonies he was automatically put in prison for life or 25 years, which is basically a life sentence. President Trump began helping the HBCUs and giving them grant money that they needed and the loans they needed so they could renovate.

You would be surprised at some of these black colleges where the dormitories need renovation, and some of them don't even have central air conditioning, but have outdated window units. You'd be surprised if you go to some of these black colleges that have not had any renovations because they don't have the money. And President Trump turned and said "what is it that you want?" And he went and saw to it that black colleges got the money that they needed—even much more than the Obama administration ever gave them. These are the things the liberal media or the Democrats will not tell you. I know about these things because I serve on his advisory board.

Some of these black colleges the president helped were also Christian colleges, and President Trump didn't deny them funding because they were Christian universities; instead, he gave them the same money as the secular schools. Tell me that's not a man who cares about the things of God. He didn't punish them because they are Christian universities, owned by the church. He gave them the same financial funding as other universities and made provisions for them to get some work done so they can offer more education for the black community. This president has made funds available for Christian universities and colleges, including the black universities and colleges that needed funding. He made provision for that. He acknowledged that when church and state did not allow Christian universities and colleges to receive the same funding as a secular school, this was not just and fair; so he leveraged it so that the Christian universities and colleges can get some of the same funding that the secular schools get. So he actually created more opportunities for individuals to go to good schools that adhere to Judeo-Christian values, as opposed to only giving funding to far-left universities that propagate anti-Christian values.

Then he turned around and he stood up for the black babies that are being aborted every day. A disproportionately high number of abortions take place in the black community, and abortion is the annihilation of black children through organizations like Planned Parenthood, which was started by a racist white woman named Margaret Sanger. Donald Trump is the first president that went to the pro-life rally to help save the babies and to stand against abortion. He stood up. He took a stand. Even though President Trump is not a perfect man, how can you not stand with this president who is standing for the things that matter most to the Lord? He needs our prayers and our votes in order to get into office for a second term. Will you stand with this president?

Many black pastors know that the Word of God says "Thou shalt not kill," but almost all of them failed to stand up with President Trump to say that we are going to save our black babies by standing up against these abortion clinics which are mostly in black communities. Abortion clinics like Planned Parenthood want to take our tax money and use it for abortions, and President Trump has been fighting to defund the abortion industry. He has said no, you're not going to take tax money from citizens that are against abortion and use it to pay for abortions. You're not going to do that, he said, because President Trump is against killing babies and using tax money from Christians to pay for it. To take tax dollars from Christians and pay for abortions to kill babies and not have Christians have anything to say about it is the most disgusting thing I have ever seen.

Donald Trump has also done many things to allow the church to have the freedom that no other president has given to any church. He has made provision for the church to be more protected from government tyranny and for the church to be elevated and given the same freedoms as the world. I serve on his advisory council, and I know that he has taken the time to make sure that the church is respected more and that it is put in a place of importance with the federal government, rather than being put under the control of the government. President Trump has worked to restore and elevate the status of the church so that it can make its own decisions according to the liberties we have under the Constitution.

President Trump has also listened and allowed people and ministers, and even black ministers, to meet with him and to talk with him about problems and disparities in their communities. He is extremely accessible, but a lot of ignorant, closed-minded leaders would rather not sit at the table with him.

President Trump also assigned Dr. Ben Carson as the Secretary of Housing and Urban Development, because black communities have had so many issues with housing, and the president wanted to put a competent black man in that position to oversee housing. President Trump felt that the black community needed to address housing from someone like Dr. Carson who knows the black community. This year at the Republican National Convention there was a feature where blacks and other minority workers from New York city public housing departments gave Donald Trump and Ben Carson a lot of credit for doing something to help poor people get better public housing after Democrats had made a big mess of things for years. Donald Trump is a man of action, but the biased media tries to hide his good deeds and report on anything they can think of that is negative.

In spite of the onslaught of negative media, all the God-fearing people in this country should simply ask the Lord to guide them in terms of what to listen to and how to vote. This next election is more critical than ever before in our nation's history because the Supreme Court is also at stake. Along with all the liberal judges that are stacked on the Supreme Court, there are already some so-called conservative judges that have been a disappointment because they have not fully upheld the constitution and have acted like liberals in some cases. Therefore we as Christians need to pray that the right person is in the White House in order to appoint the Supreme Court justices who will truly uphold our Judeo-Christian values and religious freedom. We as Christians should also pray that the next appointees to the court will truly fear God, so we won't get some wolves in sheep's clothing like in times past.

The Bible teaches us that the world loves their own, so far-left liberal leaders are going to look out for the world—not the church, not the Christians. They are not going to look out for Israel. They are not going to look out for the biblical principles that the church stands for. They are not going to look out for the best interest of every American. They are going to follow the dialogue that the world is calling for.

In John 15:18-19, Jesus said, "If the world hates you, you know that it hated Me before it hated you. If you were of the world, the world would love its own. Yet because you are not of the world, but I chose you out of the world, therefore the world hates you." Many of the far-left leaders of the world are going to look out for radical, far-left individuals or organizations that pretend to stand for freedom, but they actually call evil good and call good evil just like it says in Isaiah 5:20. They demonize all police officers, riot, and burn down the houses and businesses of innocent people. They claim to be fighting for racial justice and equality for black people, but they are treacherous outsiders who burn down black businesses and black communities or remain silent when neighborhood criminals burn down their own communities or commit black-on-black crimes.

Consequently, we need to vote for the leader that will uphold God's commandments in order to help restore law and order, and the things that President Trump has done so far are magnificent. I've never known anybody like President Trump, who has never lived in despair, but still has the level of compassion for those that are in desperation and those that are down and out. I have never ever seen any person who has been rich practically all his life to be such a hard worker like he is. I mean, he works from six in the morning till late at night every day of the week. He just tirelessly works on solving the problems in the communities, so I thank God for him and I know God put him in the White House. And he's not going anywhere until God gets through with him. But we need every person who stands for the Lord to also stand with President Trump, because he is the person God has called for this day and time. This is what Almighty God showed me.

ENDNOTES

Chapter 1: Did God Really Put Donald J. Trump in the White House?

1 Julian Glover and Ken Miguel, "Race in America: What are Structural, Institutional and Systemic Racism?", ABC 7 News, July 9, 2020, https://abc7news.com/systemic-racism-definition-structural-institutionalized-what-is/6292530/

2. Maya Rhodan, "President Obama: 'Mr. Trump Will Not Be President,'" TIME USA, LLC, February 16, 2016, https://time.com/4226736/president-obama-mr-trump-will-not-be-president/

Chapter 3: Let My People Go!

1. Paul Bedard, "Report: Illegal immigration harms blacks, robs social services from legal Americans," Washington Examiner, June 19, 2018, https://www.washingtonexaminer.com/washington-secrets/report-illegal-immigration-harms-blacks-robs-social-services-from-legal-americans

2. Paul Bedard, "Report: Illegal immigration harms blacks, robs social services from legal Americans."

3. Laurent Belsie, "Effects of Immigration on African-American Employment and Incarceration," National Bureau of Economic Research, August 14, 2020, https://www.nber.org/digest/may07/w12518.html

4. Pastor Darrell Scott, "Trump helping black communities thrive," The Delaware Gazette, Posted on November 14, 2019, https://www.delgazette.com/opinion/80155/trump-helping-black-communities-thrive

5. Gianno Caldwell, "How Trump—not Biden—has helped make black lives better," pub, July 4, 2020, https://nypost.com/2020/07/04/trump-not-biden-has-helped-make-black-lives-better/

6. Barry Latzer, "The Need to Discuss Black-on-Black Crime," National Review, December 5, 2019, https://www.nationalreview.com/magazine/2019/12/22/the-need-to-discuss-black-on-black-crime/

7. Heather Mac Donald, "There is no epidemic of fatal police shootings against unarmed Black Americans," USA Today, Published July 3, 2020, Updated July 6, 2020 https://www.usatoday.com/story/opinion/2020/07/03/police-black-killings-homicide-rates-race-injustice-column/3235072001/

8. Dan Andros, "From Prison to Full Pardon: Alice Johnson's Incredible Testimony," CBN News Podcast, August 31, 2020, https://www1.cbn.com/dailyrundown/archive/2020/08/31/from-prison-to-full-pardon-alice-johnsons-incredible-testimony

9. Alice Marie Johnson, "Alice Johnson, whose life sentence was commuted by President Donald Trump, speaks to voters at the 2020 Republican National Convention," ABC News, Aug 27, 2020, https://www.youtube.com/watch?v=ZvVdHl0kJ2o

10. Alice Marie Johnson, "Alice Johnson, whose life sentence was commuted."

11. Alice Marie Johnson, "Alice Johnson, whose life sentence was commuted."

12. Alice Marie Johnson, "Alice Johnson, whose life sentence was commuted."

Chapter 4: Whose Side Are You On?

1. Carlin Becker, "Kanye West defends supporting Trump: It's 'mental slavery' to make decisions based on race," Washington Examiner, October 05, 2019, https://www.washingtonexaminer.com/news/kanye-west-defends-supporting-trump-its-mental-slavery-to-make-decisions-based-on-race

2. Carlin Becker, "Kanye West defends supporting Trump."

3. Carlin Becker, "Kanye West defends supporting Trump."

4. "Kanye West Says Democrats Brainwash Black People, Encourage Abortion," TMZ, October 29, 2019, https://www.tmz.com/2019/10/29/kanye-west-democrats-brainwash-black-people-abortion/

5. Tufayel Ahmed, "Kanye West Says Black People Are 'Brainwashed' and Democrats Are 'Making Us Abort Our Children,'" Newsweek, October 29, 2019, https://www.newsweek.com/kanye-west-black-people-brainwashed-democrats-abortions-1468470

Chapter 6: Never Trumpers, Haters, and Traitors

1. CBN News Report about Hydroxychloroquine, Reported by Dale Hurd, The 700 Club, CBN, August 10, 2020, video, 17:58, https://www1.cbn.com/video/700club/2020/08/10/the-700-club-august-10-2020?show=700club

2. Beth LeBlanc, "Democrats plan to censure lawmaker who credited Trump for COVID-19 recovery," The Detroit News, April 23, 2020, Updated April 24, 2020, https://www.detroitnews.com/story/news/politics/2020/04/23/democrats-plan-censure-lawmaker-whitsett-credited-trump-covid-19-recovery/3010947001/

3. Amanda Woods, "Michigan Democratic lawmaker says hydroxychloroquine saved her life," New York Post, April 7, 2020, https://nypost.com/2020/04/07/michigan-democrat-says-hydroxychloroquine-saved-her-life/

4. Paul Egan, "Detroit rep says hydroxychloroquine, Trump helped save her life amid COVID-19 fight," Detroit Free Press, April 6, 2020, https://www.freep.com/story/news/local/michigan/detroit/2020/04/06/democrat-karen-whitsett-coronavirus-hydroxychloroquine-trump/2955430001/

5. Tyler Olson, "Democratic Georgia rep who endorsed Trump resigns after backlash: report," Fox News, Published April 22, 2020, https://www.foxnews.com/politics/dem-georgia-rep-who-endorsed-trump-resigns-after-backlash-report

6. Tyler Olson, "Democratic Georgia rep who endorsed Trump resigns after backlash."

7. Nick Gillespie, "Shark Tank's Kevin O'Leary Explains Donald Trump's Success," Interview with Kevin O'Leary, Reason Foundation, August 1, 2019, https://reason.com/video/shark-tanks-kevin-oleary-explains-donald-trumps-success/

8. Nick Gillespie, "Shark Tank's Kevin O'Leary Explains Donald Trump's Success."

9. Nick Gillespie, "Shark Tank's Kevin O'Leary Explains Donald Trump's Success."

10. Republican National Convention, "Former football player Herschel Walker speaks about his 'friend' Donald Trump," YouTube, August 24, 2020, https://www.youtube.com/watch?v=5Rzu8IR7pYo

11. Caleb Parke, "Herschel Walker explains he spoke at RNC because 'people don't really know Donald Trump,'" Herschel Walker interview with Laura Ingraham, Fox News, Published August 26, 2020, https://www.foxnews.com/politics/trump-rnc-herschel-walker-speech

12. Caleb Parke, "Herschel Walker explains he spoke at RNC because 'people don't really know Donald Trump.'"

Chapter 7: Who Will Stand in the Midst of the Leadership Crisis?

1. Jason Whitlock, "Whitlock: You Kneel, You Don't Play," Speak for Yourself, Fox Sports, July 20, 2018, Video, https://www.foxsports.com/watch/speak-for-yourself/video/1282054723862

2. Jason Whitlock, "Jason Whitlock slams professional sports owners for caving to Black Lives Matter's agenda," Interview by Tucker Carlson, Tucker Carlson Tonight, Fox News, Aired July 6, 2020, Video, https://www.foxnews.com/media/jason-whitlock-nfl-black-national-anthem

3. Jason Whitlock, "Jason Whitlock slams professional sports owners."

Made in the USA
Coppell, TX
09 November 2020

41043053R00059